XML

IN
LIBRARIES

EDITED BY
ROY TENNANT

Neal-Schuman Publishers, Inc.
NEW YORK   LONDON

Published by Neal-Schuman Publishers, Inc.
100 Varick Street
New York, NY 10013

Printed and bound in the United States of America.

The paper used in this publication meets the minimum requirements of American National Standard for Information Sciences—Permanence of Paper for Printed Library Materials, ANSI Z39.48–1992.⊛

Library of Congress Cataloging-in-Publication Data

XML in Libraries / Roy Tennant, editor
     p. cm.
   Includes bibliographical references and index.
   ISBN 1-55570-443-3 (alk. paper)
   1. XML (Document markup language). 2. Libraries–
Automation. I. Tennant Roy.

Z678.93.X54 X54 2002
005.7'2—dc21   2002005807

Table of Contents

List of Figures

Preface

One of the most significant developments in modern librarianship was the creation of Machine-Readable Cataloging (MARC). With the MARC format, computers could read, index, and manipulate library catalog records, thereby making card catalogs obsolete (albeit over a period of decades). More importantly, since MARC was a standard way to encode and transport bibliographic information from catalog to catalog, records could be shared between computer systems. This simple fact enabled librarians to easily create union catalogs, from small local consortia to the largest bibliographic database ever constructed.

The Extensible Markup Language (XML) has the potential to exceed the impact of MARC on librarianship. While MARC is limited to bibliographic description—and arguably a subset at that, as any archivist will tell you—XML provides a highly-effective framework for encoding anything from a bibliographic record for a book to the book itself. As the projects described here illustrate, XML can be used *now* for the most practical of applications, solve library problems, and create new opportunities. The diversity of XML-based library projects also demonstrates that our opportunities with this breakthrough technology are likely limited only by our imagination.

What makes XML such a powerful tool for library needs? Libraries constantly deal with structured information. The bibliographic records in our library catalogs are highly structured—with fields, subfields, and indicators that demarcate and identify the various parts of the record. Journals are comprised of volumes, issues, articles, letters, and a variety of other definable components. Books have authors, titles, chapters, headings, paragraphs, etc. All of these items can be encoded in XML in a manner that allows computer software to process them into other formats, extract particular parts for display or further processing, or apply transformations to produce a different display.

XML is therefore quickly becoming the standard method by which information of a variety of types is encoded, transported, and processed. Librarians, as professionals who collect, organize, provide access to, and preserve information, are finding that XML is as basic a tool to their work as a hammer is to a carpenter. The early projects described in *XML in Libraries* are exciting examples of how librarians are applying extensible markup language to library problems or using it to create new opportunities. Our hope is that it will inspire others to do the same.

Besides providing inspiration, we also attempt to provide enough information about each project so that you can envision how to do it yourself, or perhaps even follow the recipe. *XML in Libraries* is divided into seven major library applications that XML is already profoundly influencing: library catalogs, interlibrary loan, cataloging and indexing, and building collections, databases, data migration, and systems interoperability. Innovators in these key areas each tackle a different aspect. Each chapter follows a standard organization, describing the project goals and justifications, project description, problems and challenges, successes and failures, plans, tips and advice, implications, contacts, and links and resources. We describe how specific tasks were accomplished, drop in snippets of code when they are particularly useful or illustrative, provide contact information, and list links to further resources. Our hope is that by providing such details you will be able to start farther along than we did, and perhaps go further as a result.

Application I, "Using XML in Library Catalog Records," shows how XML can be used to update and manipulate MARC records. As the Stanford project in Chapter 1, "Updating MARC Records with XMLMARC," demonstrates, an XML-based infrastructure can free a library from the constraints of your library systems vendor and provide a flexible, platform-independent system for maintaining MARC records that can be enhanced or refined with a minimal amount of effort. We also explore how the Web and XML may be breathing new life into Z39.50 as a method to query databases. Chapter 2, "Searching and Retrieving XML Records via the Web," highlights a project that uses Z39.50 capabilities that are so new they are not yet fully standardized.

Application II explores "Using XML for Interlibrary Loan." ILL is an activity that seems to call out for XML, since most ILL systems are Rube Goldberg-style conglomerations of automated systems and manual procedures. XML, as a standard method for encoding, transferring, interpreting, and processing information can be the glue that ties it all together. Chapter 3, "Improving Interlibrary Loan with XML," illustrates just how this can occur in the author's description of how the library at Oregon State University did just that in their interlibrary loan department.

The use of XML to improve searching of archival finding aids, to catalog Web sites, and to create semi-automated indexing of documents are some specific examples of using XML to support various kinds of searching, as described in Application III, "Using XML for Cataloging & Indexing." Chapter 4 explores "Harnessing Oracle and XT for Finding Aid Dissemination and Search." Chapter 5 investigates "Creating a Unified E-Government Portal using XML." Chapter 6 examines "Expediting the Work of the Indexer with XML."

Since XML was born out of the marriage of SGML (Standard Generalized Markup Language, frequently used for encoding books), and the Web, it should come as no surprise that libraries are using XML to move parts of their collections online. Application IV is "Using XML to Build Collections." The examples provided for building digital library collections show some of the potentials for the technology as well as some of the problems being encountered. Chapter 7, "Using XML to Federate Collections: The Legacy Tobacco Documents Library," and Chapter 8, "Publishing Books Online at eSchlorship," also show the differences in these projects illustrating that there are likely many paths to success.

Application V addresses "Using XML in Databases." They are of course important to libraries, and increasingly the library catalog is but one of several databases that a library may need to create and maintain. Chapter 9's "Building XML Databases with Zope and Castor" compares and contrasts two XML-based database systems for creating library services in the Databases section.

Although XML excels at being able to move information forward over time as requirements change, Application VI, "Using XML for Data Migration," has more to do with getting legacy information, or documents created in standard word processors, into XML for better persistence and enhanced usability. Chapter 10, "Migrating Native Law Cases from HTML to XML," and Chapter 11, "Transforming Word Processing Documents into XML: Electronic Scholarly Publishing at the University of Michigan," search this stimulating area. Over the next several years, we must become very good at such migrations so that we can take the best advantage that structured markup has to provide.

Application VII, "Using XML for Systems Interoperability," describes how XML is being used to provide interoperability between disparate systems. Chapter 12, " Encoding Digital Objects with METS," and Chapter 13, "Integrating Systems with XML-based Web Services," demonstrate how XML is rapidly becoming the platform of choice for sharing information between systems—whether you are Microsoft or the University of Saskatchewan. The systems we rely upon in libraries will increasingly be constructed as components that can easily share information with many other components to accomplish what needs to be done. XML will be the carrier syntax for this information.

Through these practical, real-world projects you will discover that XML provides an easy and yet powerful way to encode, transfer, process, and store data of all types. In addition, XML-encoded data is easily read by humans, which means if all else fails you will not be left with your data trapped in an outdated format from which no recovery is possible.

Although these projects and others not described in *XML in Libraries* show that libraries are already using XML for production services, we are still in the early stages of using XML in libraries. Much experimentation is taking place, and will continue to take place as we discover what works well and what doesn't. But even now, it's clear that XML will not only be a part of our future, it will often be how we get there.

ROY TENNANT
Editor

Application I

USING XML IN LIBRARY CATALOG RECORDS

IN LIBRARIES

The cornerstone of library automation remains the integrated library system. But despite its central role in providing information about a library's collections to its clientele, what a library can accomplish with its ILS is often limited by it. That is, if a different kind of report is required than that provided by the system, a library must request an enhancement from the automated systems vendor from which it purchased the system, and often must wait a significant length of time (and/or pay a significant development fee) to get the requested enhancement. If, on the other hand, data about the library's collection could be extracted in a structured and easily processed way (e.g., XML), then many things become possible.

CHAPTER 1

In Chapter 1, "Updating MARC Records with XMLMARC," Kevin Clarke describes how Stanford has created an infrastructure to easily do what previously would have required costly and time-consuming enhancements from an automated systems vendor. But much better than that, Stanford has done this with an eye toward helping us all do it as well. XMLMARC is a set of specifications and software that virtually any library can use. There are many useful projects described in this book, but this chapter alone could easily be worth the price, as it most assuredly can save you a significant amount of money and time.

CHAPTER 2

The second chapter, "Searching and Retrieving XML Records via the Web," is Theo van Veen's approach to catalog systems from the user's perspective. This project makes catalog information more easily discoverable and usable to Web browsers or, to be more accurate, to anything (be it software or human) that can send a properly formulated Web request. Although the Koninklijke Bibliotheek is currently using this system with the one Web browser that supports XSL, one could also imagine a software program (such as a Web CGI) taking advantage of such functionality. The bottom line is that work such as that at Koninklijke Bibliotheek may help make all of our catalogs more open to querying from a variety of sources while also providing a result that can easily be parsed and displayed by software according to individual specifications.

1

Updating MARC Records with XMLMARC

Kevin S. Clarke
Stanford University

BACKGROUND

The Lane Medical Library Medlane/XMLMARC project's goal is to experiment with ways to better integrate library information and the information resources of the World Wide Web. Today's patrons prefer to search integrated online resources; many will even ignore resources that segregate themselves from online integrated search tools. We believe that library information is in danger of becoming marginalized unless librarians adopt a more universal format for sharing their data. In 1999, Lane Library addressed this problem by releasing XMLMARC, free software that converts MARC, or Machine Readable Cataloging, into XML.

While converting MARC into XML is the main purpose of the XMLMARC program, we recognize that most libraries use proprietary library systems and that every mainstream library system, at this point, uses MARC as its input and output format. As a transitional solution, we have experimented with leveraging the flexibility and simplicity of XML to simplify the day-to-day processing of MARC records. This second aspect of the Medlane/XMLMARC project has led to the creation of MARCUTL, the MARC Update and Transformation Language.

This transformation language, expressed in XML, is an attempt to describe systematically the types of changes that could be made to a MARC record. Using a MARCUTL file and the XMLMARC program, updates and transformations can be made to a batch of MARC records without having to rely on in-house programming or on a library system vendor's willingness to customize its proprietary MARC loading or extraction process. We believe that by capitalizing on the strengths of XML, MARC record manipulation can be made easier.

PROJECT GOALS AND JUSTIFICATION

The goals of the Medlane/XMLMARC project have evolved over the course of its development. The project started with the following goals:

- flexibly transforming MARC records into XML based on a user-supplied mapping between the MARC and XML formats,
- allowing for experimentation with different XML formats to determine how to better structure library information, and
- ensuring the usefulness of MARC records by transporting and possibly storing them in an open, software-independent manner.

Although there are several programs that enable librarians to convert MARC records into XML, the use of XML to structure and represent the full set of library information is still in its infancy. In 1999, when the first version of XMLMARC was written, care was taken to ensure that the mapping language was flexible enough to accommodate almost any type of transformation. Initially, this was done by embedding logical statements, expressed in a syntax similar to the Java programming language, into the transformation map. Recently, however, we decided to rewrite the map language so that it uses XML to express the logic of the changes. In the process, we included a vocabulary for describing transformations between two MARC records.

With the development of MARCUTL, the project's goals evolved to include the following:

- creating a way to perform batch updates on MARC records without having to rely on custom programming or on a library system vendor's assistance,
- ensuring the longevity of this solution by using a flexible, platform-independent system architecture, and
- developing an extensible solution that can be enhanced or refined as needed with a minimal amount of effort.

Maintaining a process that performs local batch updating on MARC records can be a time-consuming process. Before a recent shift in hardware platforms, Lane Medical Library had developed five separate software programs that performed a variety of updates on the MARC records that entered and exited our library system. With the change of hardware, however, we took advantage of the opportunity to rewrite these programs into one single program using a platform-independent programming language. When considering the requirements of a new MARC batch update program, we valued flexibility as its most important feature.

Our previous programs, which served us well for 15 years, were customized to act based on instructions in the programming code. When we wanted to search for the occurrence of a particular field and perform an action on the record based on its occurrence, we would have to request that one of the library's programmers write a new program or a new method in an old program to accomplish this task. Although this worked well, it was an expensive and time-consuming way to maintain the MARC update process.

The alternative we chose was to use XML as a way to describe the transformations we wanted to make to the MARC record. By choosing XML, we eliminated the need for customized programming every time we want to add a new transformation to our record update process. By using a MARCUTL file that describes the update, the XMLMARC program can make the necessary additions to the process without having to be modified. As long as the transformation file is well formed and conforms to the MARCUTL DTD, the XMLMARC program knows how to process the new additions.

PROJECT DESCRIPTION

The MARC to XML conversion part of the XMLMARC program has been described in other places, so only a little space will be devoted to it in this chapter. Stated simply, the program allows for MARC records to be converted into XML records based on a user-supplied map. Optionally, one of the default output formats embedded in the program may be selected. By selecting a MARC file and an output format, users can generate XML in Medlane's format, a custom format, the Library of Congress's format, the Open Archive Initiative's format, or the format of MARC.pm, a Perl program for converting MARC into XML.

In addition, the program's output may be customized so that it writes the XML records into one large file, ideal for loading into a database, or into many individual files, better suited for indexing by a free-text search engine. Improvements have been made to the program's original design that make it easier to use. The only other thing a library needs in order to run the program is a computer running a Java Virtual Machine (JVM). JVMs are available for Windows, Macintosh, and UNIX machines. For more information, see the Links and Resources section at the end of this chapter.

The MARCUTL part of the XMLMARC project allows us to adapt our batch record updating process dynamically without having to write new programming code. It does this by relying on the XMLMARC program's ability to process XML, specifically the MARCUTL XML file describing the types of changes we want to make to our MARC records as they are imported into and exported out of our integrated library system. Whenever we need to update to our import/export process, we add another structure of XML elements to our file.

For instance, the following example checks a MARC record for the existence of a value at a particular byte position in the leader. If the program finds a match, the value of that byte position is changed accordingly. In the following case, if XMLMARC finds a MARC record that has the obsolete value 'p' in byte 7 of the leader, the program automatically updates the record by putting an 'm' in that position.

```xml
<field tag="000">
    <match name="RLIN: Updates obsolete value for analytics" recordStatus="new">
        <pattern>
            <bytes range="07">p</bytes>
        </pattern>
        <result action="replace" targetRecord="self">
            <actionBytes>m</actionBytes>
        </result>
    </match>
</field>
```

To make the transformation language as general as possible, we have tried to isolate the types of changes one might want to make to a MARC record. At this time, we are using eight types of updates: add, copy, move, replace, burst, delete, normalize, and reorder. Some are self-explanatory: an "add" action will add a new field to a record if the program is able to match the pattern in the pattern element. Others may not be apparent at first glance. For instance, "burst" will create variable fields based on the occurrence of a byte or byte range in one of the record's control fields.

```xml
<field tag="000">
    <match name="Lane: Burst 655 values from 000:06-07" recordStatus="new">
        <pattern>
            <bytes range="06-07"/>
        </pattern>
        <result action="burst" targetRecord="self">
            <case value="am">
                <actionField tag="655" indicators="17">
                    <actionSubfield name="a">Book</actionSubfield>
                </actionField>
            </case>
            <case value="?c">
                <actionField tag="655" indicators="17">
                    <actionSubfield name="a">Collection</actionSubfield>
                </actionField>
            </case>
            <case value="as ab">
```

```
        <actionField tag="655" indicators="17">
            <actionSubfield name="a">Serial</actionSubfield>
        </actionField>
      </case>
    </result>
  </match>
</field>
```

In the above example, XMLMARC looks at the sixth and seventh bytes of the MARC record's leader. It compares what it finds with the values of the case elements in the result structure. The first case is a straightforward example. If bytes six and seven are "am" then a 655 field with the indicators value of 17 is added to the record. An "a" subfield with the value "Book" is then added to that field.

As the second and third cases show, there is some flexibility in describing the types of patterns for which the program will search. In the second result case, XMLMARC will try to match on any record that has a "c" in byte position seven. The question mark in the sixth byte position is a wildcard allowing for any match. Likewise, a case can search for several different possibilities. In the third case, a new "Serial" 655 field is created if bytes six and seven contain "as" or "ab."

Wildcards can also be used on components of the MARC record. The program will match patterns in any 1xx field, expressed in MARCUTL as 1??. In addition, subfield names and field indicators can be given wildcard values if needed. For example, the following MARCUTL extract will delete fields by looking for the occurrence of any subfield in a specified field.

```
<field tag="222">
  <match name="Lane: delete key title; rely on LC if needed" recordStatus="new">
    <pattern>
      <subfield name="?"/>
    </pattern>
    <result action="delete" targetRecord="self">
      <actionField tag="222"/>
    </result>
  </match>
</field>
```

For XMLMARC to act intelligently on a MARC record, there are several filters that determine which matches are applied to a given MARC record. The first distinction we make is whether the batch update is acting on exported records or records waiting to be imported. Secondly, we limit the types of actions performed to the type of MARC record being processed. For instance, in the following example the matches in the MARCUTL file are only applied to monographic bibliographic records waiting to be imported. Lastly, we set the source of the records as an argument at runtime.

```
<transformation>
    <marc source="Lane" processing="import">
        <record format="mono" type="bib">
            <field tag="110">
                <match name="Obsolete: U.S. —> United States" recordStatus="new">
                    <pattern>
                        <subfield name="a">*U.S.*</subfield>
                    </pattern>
                    <result action="replace" targetRecord="self">
                        <actionSubfield name="a">United States</actionSubfield>
                    </result>
                </match>
                <match name="Obsolete: U.[ ]S. —> United States" recordStatus="new">
                    <pattern>
                        <subfield name="a">*U. S.*</subfield>
                    </pattern>
                    <result action="replace" targetRecord="self">
                        <actionSubfield name="a">United States</actionSubfield>
                    </result>
                </match>
            </field>
        </record>
    </marc>
</transformation>
```

The above extract from a MARCUTL file updates the obsolete terms U.S. and U. S. in a 110 field of an imported record whose source is Lane. If all the filters match a MARC record in the file being processed, any occurrence of U.S. or U. S. in the 110 field will be replaced by the correct format, United States.

If any of the filters do not match the record in memory, the update will not be attempted. Obviously, due to the size constraints of this chapter, a full description of the MARCUTL language is not possible. For a more detailed description and MARCUTL tutorial, visit the XMLMARC Web page.

PROBLEMS AND CHALLENGES,
SUCCESSES AND FAILURES

We learned many things with the initial release of the XMLMARC program, both about how libraries are using XML and about what type of libraries are experimenting with it. Suggestions we received from users helped us redesign the program to improve the user interface and to allow for more flexibility in controlling the output of the XML. Despite the changes there are still challenges ahead for the development of XMLMARC.

Perhaps the biggest problem facing developers is how to simply express search concepts which, when working with MARC records, can sometimes get quite complex. The challenge in working with MARCUTL is to isolate the particular pieces of logic involved with a desired record update. Sometimes a "single" update is accomplished in two or more steps.

One solution, which has been integrated into the most recent version, is the ability to use regular expressions in the text portion of subfield pattern matches. At this stage, implementation of this is sketchy at best, but there are several cases in which Lane uses regular expressions to isolate fields that resisted retrieval by the concepts of the MARCUTL language alone. Hopefully, in the future, MARCUTL will be modified to support regular expression matches in a simple XML form.

In addition, there are parts of the XMLMARC code that are not optimally designed. Our emphasis in writing XMLMARC was to keep it as modular as possible so that new features or bug fixes could be completed with minimal extra effort. However, given the limited time frame for the project's development, there were some compromises made in the program's overall design. Now that our new integrated library system is working and XMLMARC is successfully performing our updates, the author hopes to revise these portions of the code.

The MARCUTL part of the XMLMARC project has also succeeded nicely in that it has produced a truly useful XML product that will save the library money over time. By generalizing the types of actions one might make on a MARC record and creating a way to describe those actions to the program, we believe, XMLMARC has reduced the need for custom programming in the future. As the update language grows, programmers will be needed to update the map processing code, but the next time Lane Medical Library wants to add a new update to its processing, cataloging staff can add the change to the MARCUTL file with relative ease.

The main challenge, at this point, is to strengthen the MARC Update and Transformation Language so that it robustly handles almost any kind of MARC update that a library might want to do. We also continue our work on a new XMLMARC MARC record schema, this time focusing on describing what a library record should look like rather than depending so much on the current structure of MARC. We expect to release the first draft to coincide with the publication of this book.

PLANS

We believe MARCUTL and the XMLMARC program will benefit other libraries that either cannot afford to hire their own programmers or who wish to augment their batch updating process efficiently. To make this possible, we are releasing the XMLMARC software and corresponding MARC update language under the GNU General Public License, a "free software" license. The release should correspond with the publication of this book.

Feedback regarding the usefulness of the MARCUTL language is welcome and will be instrumental in allowing us to make XMLMARC more generally useful to the library community. We also welcome the participation of librarians and library programmers interested in improving the Java code that processes MARCUTL. If you are interested, please contact either the author or someone at the project's Web site.

By collaborating with other librarians interested in developing a set of free tools for all libraries to use, we hope to foster community and simplify the tasks that libraries and librarians perform on a daily basis. We believe that in the end, our patrons benefit by our cooperation. For information on other library-specific free software projects, visit the Open Source Software for Librarians (OSS4LIB) Web site.

TIPS AND ADVICE (LESSONS LEARNED)

The MARCUTL portion of the Medlane/XMLMARC project developed in response to a pragmatic need: to process our weekly batch updates, we required a program that would not require a lot of maintenance and updating. For this task, XML seemed like the perfect fit. XML's flexibility and platform-independence ensures we will be able to use XMLMARC with any system's software and on any mainstream hardware platform we choose. In addition, XML's extensible nature and the object-oriented design of the programming code ensure that we will be able to make additions with a minimal amount of effort.

However, creating a transformation language in response to a very well-defined set of objectives does influence certain design decisions. Although we wanted to make our mapping language as generic as possible, we sometimes made decisions based on what would make the process of updating our records easier. This solution works fine for us but, as we learned, sometimes limits the usefulness of the program. For instance, when we first used the XMLMARC program, we used it to perform the same MARC updates we had made with our previous programs. After awhile, the ability to easily add new changes encouraged us to create new maps. Very quickly, we found out that we needed to include regular expressions in our patterns. While this wasn't necessary for our earlier updates, we concluded we could not do without this feature for many of our later maps.

During the course of MARCUTL's development, we learned that being able to do one simple procedure often leads to the desire to do something a bit more complex. Now that we have finished the first version of the transformation language and are successfully using XMLMARC to perform our daily batch updates, we plan to return to the task of refining the markup language's expressiveness. We welcome participation in this effort.

IMPLICATIONS

XMLMARC was created to experiment with the reformatting of Lane Library's MARC records into XML records. The Document Type Definitions (DTDs) of the first release were a proof of concept, demonstrating that the transformation could be done, but they were not what we would recommend as the ideal data structures for library information. The second version of these DTDs, now released as a RELAX NG schema, attempts to better organize the library's catalog data. We hope it will stimulate discussion in the library community and that others will contribute to its improvement. Schemata or DTDs for other units of library information (for instance, circulation data, interlibrary loan data, etc.) are areas for future work.

The development of MARCUTL and the ability to modify MARC records with the XMLMARC program suggest some new directions for the Medlane project. Enabling librarians who do not program to be able to make batch changes to MARC records without relying either on the search and replace functions of large integrated library systems or on a library programmer may give smaller libraries greater control over their data. This could enable them to customize library data to their patrons' needs. To make the MARCUTL language more accessible to those not familiar with XML, we are working on an editor that would not require that the librarian know XML to be able to edit the transformation map.

Lastly, once MARC records are reformatted, what does a library do with them? Because XML is not a library-specific format, like MARC, there are a wide range of tools that may be used to store and query the records. The Medlane project has been investigating relational databases, object-oriented databases, native XML databases, and free-text search engines for the storage and retrieval of our records. We are also working on two XML tools that enable librarians to edit their bibliographic and authority records without having to know XML. We plan to make these tools available once we believe they will be useful to the library community.

CONTACTS

Kevin S. Clarke
Digital Information Systems Developer
Lane Medical Library, Stanford University
300 Pasteur Drive, L109
Stanford, CA 94305
ksclarke@stanford.edu
(650) 498-6016

Dick R. Miller
Systems Librarian, Head of Technical Services
Lane Medical Library, Stanford University
300 Pasteur Drive, L109
Stanford, CA 94305
dick@stanford.edu
(650) 725-4615

LINKS AND RESOURCES

Medlane Project
medlane.stanford.edu
The Medlane page is the Medlane/XMLMARC project's main page. It contains information about the XMLMARC program and the new Medlane XML schema and serves as a general introduction to the project in addition to providing contact information for those involved with the project. Visitors interested in learning more about XML and librarianship should consult the online bibliography.

XMLMARC
xmlmarc.stanford.edu
This is a direct link to the XMLMARC program's homepage. Links from this page point to screen shots of the program, a tutorial, and a mailing list set up to provide assistance to those interested in processing their MARC records with XMLMARC.

XML: Libraries' Strategic Opportunity

www.libraryjournal.com/xml.asp

In this article, Dick Miller explains some of the advantages of XML and suggests that librarians adopt the XML format. One of the first articles specifically related to XML and librarianship, it is a very good introduction to XML for librarians.

Open Source Software for Librarians (OSS4LIB)

www.oss4lib.org

An extremely useful site that gathers information about free library software. Not all of the software is XML related but some is, such as the MARC.pm program mentioned in the chapter. In addition to providing information about library software, there are a few articles related to the development and selection of software for libraries.

MARC 21 Documentation

lcweb.loc.gov/marc/marcdocz.html

This official MARC21 site documents the MARC format. Any librarian interested in writing a custom XMLMARC map should visit this site for assistance with the MARC format.

Java Virtual Machine (JVM)

java.sun.com/j2se/1.3/jre/

A Java Virtual Machine, also known as a Java Runtime Environment, is needed to run the XMLMARC program. There are many available. A Java Virtual Machine sits on top of the computer's operating system and executes Java programs. If you have a question about installing a JVM on your machine, feel free to ask the XMLMARC mailing list.

XMLSOFTWARE

www.xmlsoftware.com

This collection of XML tools includes editors, databases, search engines, and other transformation tools. This site contains commercial and open source products.

XMLMARC Mailing List
lists.sourceforge.net/lists/listsinfo/medland-xmlmarc
A mailing list maintained by the Medlane project to support users of the XMLMARC program.

2

Searching and Retrieving XML Records via the Web

Theo van Veen
Koninklijke Bibliotheek

BACKGROUND

The Koninklijke Bibliotheek (KB) has been using XML for storage and retrieval of bibliographic records since late 1998. This XML database contains about 20 catalogs of different collections, of which the OPAC is the largest. This infrastructure is used for the access of metadata by different projects and will also be part of the European Library project. Access to this information is provided by several Web applications written in Perl, which led to increasing danger of divergence. To standardize the access to this XML infrastructure, it was decided that the output would also be XML, and standard Web requests would be supported.

At the same time, the Z39.50 implementers group began a similar initiative called "Z39.50 Next Generation." Under this umbrella two standards were proposed: (1) Search and Retrieve via the Web (SRW), based on the use of Simple Object Access Protocol (SOAP), and (2) Search and Retrieve via URLs (SRU). The main goal behind this initiative was to get rid of some of the complexity of Z39.50 and lower the implementation barrier. Responses to requests were to be output in XML only. The resemblance to the KB standard was such that the KB decided to conform to this ZNG initiative and will start supporting SRU.

KB support for SRW will depend on the external adoption of both SRU and SRW. In this project, however, the focus is completely on SRU.

PROJECT GOALS AND JUSTIFICATION

The goals of this project are to:

- create a single standardized entrance for search and retrieval of XML records for different KB collections in such a way that Web developers can create user interfaces using XSL only, and
- conform to new international standards with respect to search and retrieval.

Searching databases that are accessible via the Web is usually done via HTML forms. These forms generate a request (GET, expressed as a URL, or POST) that might be very similar for different databases. The response is in most cases HTML, but on the server side it would be just as easy to return XML instead of HTML; for example, replace "Title: xyz" with "<title>xyz</title>." The client would handle the presentation of this XML by means of XSL. The use of this combination of URL input and XML output for different databases helps KB achieve standardization.

The conventional way to access distributed bibliographic databases is by means of the Z39.50 protocol, which is quite complex and requires specific software. Users commonly access a Web gateway that connects them to distributed databases by Z39.50. These databases are in most cases also directly accessible via a Web interface. If an XML response is possible, the Z39.50 gateway can be bypassed. This requires that the requesting URL and the response in XML comply to a commonly accepted standard.

The SRU protocol, then, provides a simple yet powerful method for querying databases in a standard way. Such a search-and-retrieval interface will have a very low implementation barrier because it can be based on existing technology: it is nothing more than standardization of the URL parameters and the XML output from an existing system. The server does

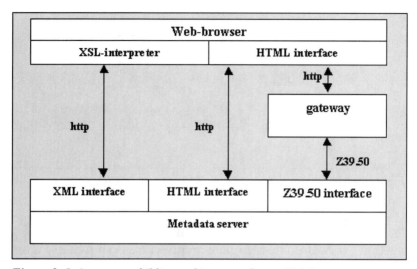

Figure 2–1. *Access to a bibliographic server from a Web browser:*
conventional (middle), standardized via Z39.50 (right) or via XML-SRU
(left)

not require any of the Z39.50 complexity, and the client is reduced to a simple style sheet interpreted by a Web browser (see
Figure 2–1).

PROJECT DESCRIPTION

KB bibliographic records come from different sources: from the
library catalog, from internal databases, and from some European national libraries. There are a number of native formats
involved, and different algorithms for retrieval and conversion.
All records are stored in XML format in an Oracle database.
Records that describe KB materials conform to the KB DTD, but
the XML infrastructure also accommodates records with other
schemata.

  All XML records are indexed in a single index (in the future there will be several indexes), and all the words from each
tag occur in the index twice: once as a keyword and once with
a prefix that consists of the name of the end node in the record
tree that contains this word. For example, a record with an XML
tag <author>smith</author> may be found by searching for

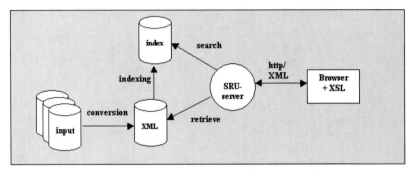

Figure 2–2. *Architecture of the KB search-and-retrieval infrastructure*

"smith" or "author:smith." The index engine currently being used is AltaVista. The complete architecture is shown in Figure 2–2.

The search-and-retrieval part is a Perl CGI script that takes the URL parameters as input and sends out a search query to the AltaVista server or a record request to the Oracle database. The response is transformed to an XML record that contains navigational information and zero or more bibliographic records. This Perl script is in fact the SRU server; the input parameters and the XML output are almost identical to specifications of the SRU protocol. This protocol is still under development; therefore, the KB implementation does support features that are not yet agreed on.

The standard request parameters are:

- the query
- a result set name
- starting record
- maximum number of records
- record schema

Parameters used in the KB implementation that are not part of the standard are:

- sort field (to have the results sorted by the server)
- link to a style sheet (to be put in the header of the XML response to be recognized by the browser)

An example query URL is:

http://www.kb.nl/cgi srw.pl?query=title:test&recordSchema=dc_record&maximum
Records=20

A simple example response is shown below.

```
<zng:searchRetrieveResponse xmlns:zng="urn:z3950:zng_prototype1">
    <zng:resultSetReference>
        <zng:resultSetName>20011018.126.kqf</zng:resultSetName>
    </zng:resultSetReference>
    <zng:totalHits>2</zng:totalHits>
    <zng:records>
        <zng:record>
            <zng:schema>kb_caption</zng:schema>
            <zng:recordData>
                <title>This is a test title</title>
                <author>Smith, John</author>
            </zng:recordData>
        </zng:record>
        <zng:record>
            <zng:schema>kb_caption</zng:schema>
            <zng:recordData>
                <title>This is another test title</title>
                <author>Jones, John</author>
            </zng:recordData>
        </zng:record>
    </zng:records>
</zng:searchRetrieveResponse>
```

In our implementation we assume that nonstandard extensions are ignored by those clients and servers that are not capable of interpreting or processing these extensions. A server
may ignore nonstandard URL parameters and a client (the style
sheet) may ignore nonstandard XML tags. On the other hand,
clients and servers should not require information that is not
part of the standard.

The result of this approach is that it is possible to add local
functionality without conflicting with the standard and without losing interoperability. Extra local functionality is only available with the combination of a local client and server, but it
might be a benefit for others when they implement this functionality as an extra option.

A very convenient extension is that the server returns the requesting parameters. This makes the response self-explanatory, and there is no need to keep session context. The SRU standard as is being discussed now does not (yet) allow this flexible approach.

The query syntax and the record schema of retrieved records are not yet standardized. The KB implementation uses a query syntax with index types as prefix (like author:smith), uses brackets to specify order of operation, and uses the keywords "and," "or," and "not" to perform Boolean operations. The output is specified by a URL parameter; in the KB implementation, valid record schemata are kb_record, kb_caption, dc_record, and dc_caption. The first two are internally used record schemata and the latter two are Dublin Core record schemata (full and short).

Architectures

On the retrieval side there are several possible architectures or use scenarios, which are shown in Figure 2–3. The first scenario is that a browser is used for transforming the XML response by means of an XSL style sheet as specified in the header of the XML record. This requires Internet Explorer and will be used for the conventional access of the XML infrastructure at the KB. Web developers will develop different style sheets for different collections based on the SRU specifications with the KB extensions.

The right-hand scenario in Figure 2–3 is that a gateway provides plain HTML to a standard Web browser and accesses the SRU server by means of HTTP/XML. This is the configuration we have in mind for accessing a mixed environment of SRU/SRW targets and Z39.50 targets. There are, however, no gateways yet that support both protocols.

The middle scenario is considered the most promising. The user may specify his own XSL style sheet and can access different SRU databases of his own choice. A very simple HTML page that sends out a query to different targets will do the job. This is the basic concept for a local—even personalized—portal.

Such a local portal can be an HTML page with an input field

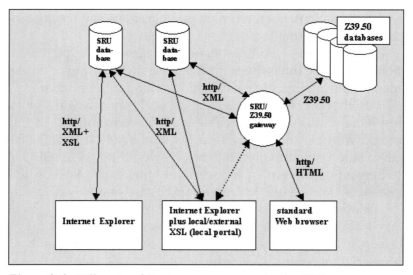

Figure 2–3. *Different architectures or use scenarios for SRU*

for a query and a fixed number of selectable targets to which the query is being sent. In this project a much better approach was used: the list of targets consist of XML records describing the targets, and these XML records are bundled as if this was an SRU response. A style sheet is being used to transform this list of targets to a search page. This is a **very important** issue: in this way SRU targets that are found with the SRU protocol may form a new list of searchable SRU targets.

In the middle option, the dotted arrow toward the gateway is not part of any known project, but is there to illustrate that Z39.50 gateways could also provide an SRU interface to a Web browser. This would stimulate integration of Z39.50 and SRU and allow adoption of the SRU standard without losing previous Z39.50 investments.

PROBLEMS AND CHALLENGES, SUCCESSES AND FAILURES

Since these SRU and SRW standards are still under development, they are a moving target and the implementation needs continuous adjustment. On the other hand, the experience from a current implementation provides suggestions and recommendations for this standard.

Problems arose because standardization and implementation aspects are interwoven, and partners with different implementations in mind have a different vision for the standard.

Another problem is the strong dependency between a given implementation and the technological environment. In our project we are leaning considerably on Internet Explorer for the client-side transformation of XML. It would be preferable not to depend on a specific product, but in the case of Web browsers, this would be too severe a limitation for our project.

Related to the dependency on Internet Explorer is a security issue. Internet Explorer does not automatically allow crossplatform combination of XSL and XML, as this is subject to restrictions and the security settings in the user's browser. That means that when offering a portal function that combines the XML from one site with the XSL from another site, the user may be requested to change these security settings or copy the relevant files to his own workstation.

Although the project goals form the justification of this project, there are two challenges that we hope will become important spin-offs or catalysts:

- It allows for the use of personal style sheets to access different collections, which will serve as personal portals.
- It allows for easy incorporation of collection-level descriptions, as search, retrieval, and navigation can be easily integrated.

Successes include the fact that internally our search-and-retrieve implementations will converge to a single service, and that interface design can be completely independent.

PLANS

Future plans depend partly on external developments. The phases that I expect in the development of search and retrieval of bibliographic data are:

- adoption of SRU by the library community

- development of combined Z39.50 and SRU/SRW gateways
- development of personal portals
- standardization of representing bibliographic records in XML (schemas)
- implementation of SRW

These phases will not strictly follow one after another: there will be some mutual dependencies. Adoption of SRU depends on its usability, and so gateways that support SRU are needed. Personal portals will eventually partly replace gateways as the adoption of SRU has exceeded some critical mass.

In the KB we will, after implementation of SRU for internal use and for the European Library test bed, concentrate on the standardization of bibliographic records. It is expected that the development of personal portals will be the result of individual initiatives.

We will let the implementation of SRW depend on the general adoption of SRW, which we expect to be strongly related to the integration of ".net" services in Web browsers.

TIPS AND ADVICE (LESSONS LEARNED)

Using a production environment when trying out new ideas is helpful. The need for internal standardization, the need for fixing specifications for the European Library test bed, and the chance of letting this directly interact with a standard under development resulted in an effective approach with immediate feedback and therefore fast results.

IMPLICATIONS

This project offers a next step toward integrating search and retrieval into navigation, in that SRU search results can be collection-level descriptions, which can themselves be used to initiate a search of those collections.

Google-type searches miss the deep-linking possibilities into databases. Z39.50 allows distributed searches in Z39.50 targets, but this is limited to the selections of targets that are offered by

Z39.50 gateways. With SRU, however, a two-step approach becomes possible: first search the targets that match certain search criteria, then send out a distributed new search to the targets that are the result of the first query.

CONTACTS

Theo van Veen
Research and Development
Koninklijke Bibliotheek
P.O. Box 90407
NL-2509 LK The Hague

LINKS AND RESOURCES

The ZING—Z39.50 International Next Generation
www.loc.gov/z3950/agency/zing/
ZING refers to a number of initiatives for evolving Z39.50 into a more mainstream protocol. The goal is to lower the barriers to implementation with respect to Z39.50 while preserving the good aspects of it. The record and response syntax will be XML.

The KB SRU service
redbelly.kb.nl/cgi-zoek/srw.pl?
This is a base URL for testing the Search and Retrieval service via URLs of the KB. At the time of this writing, the service was not yet available as a production service.

The KB-DTD
www.kb.nl/kb/sbo/catalogus/kb.dtd
The KB-DTD is the general DTD for the current XML resources in this project. Various collections will either use the general KB-DTD or have their own DTD specified.

Dublin Core Metadata Initiative
www.dublincore.org
The Dublin Core prescribes the minimal fields for bibliographic objects. In this project we propose Dublin Core as a standard schema for exchanging metadata besides a local schema. This

site also provides an overview of application profiles, some of which might be relevant for this project.

The European Library project
www.europeanlibrary.org
In the framework of the European Library project, one of the work packages will focus on testing the integration of Z39.50 and XML/HTTP for the access of bibliographic services.

Application II

USING XML FOR
INTERLIBRARY LOAN

XML IN LIBRARIES

In an age of digital information, the infrastructure that allows a library user to ask for and receive a book or journal article from a distant library has never been more important. Greater cooperation among libraries on a regional, national, and even international basis leads to easier patron discovery of books they never knew existed. Many libraries discover that increased information about available items leads to greater volumes of interlibrary loan requests.

Meanwhile, libraries are often ill-equipped to deal with these additional requests. The system's infrastructure for requesting, filling, and recording ILL transactions is often arcane and inefficient. Even the process of sending a request out to be fulfilled may require retyping bibliographic information, even though it exists in computerized form in the library catalog.

CHAPTER 3

Chapter 3, Kyle Banerjee's "Improving Interlibrary Loan with XML" presents a practical solution. XML can be used productively to link the disparate systems that must communicate in order to fulfill interlibrary loan requests.

3

Improving Interlibrary Loan with XML

Kyle Banerjee
Oregon State Library

BACKGROUND

On a typical day, Oregon State University (OSU) fills between 50 and 100 interlibrary loan requests from other libraries. Despite the use of specialized interlibrary loan software and a bibliographic utility, processing incoming requests involves a great deal of time and manual labor. As OSU increases reliance on resource sharing to combat the challenges posed by rising publishing costs, the demand for interlibrary loan services has been growing faster than resources to pay for those services. By automating manual tasks such as recording location and availability information for requested items, generating billing information, and sorting requests in call number order to facilitate retrieval from the shelves, OSU hopes to save time and money while reducing error rates.

Since 1998, OSU had used a locally developed program known as InterLibrary Loan Automatic Search and Print (ILL ASAP) that searched the catalog for location and availability information of requested materials. Although ILL ASAP saved a great deal of labor, it crashed when system updates resulted in changes to the menus or screens in the catalog. To complicate matters, the 16-bit telnet client that ILL ASAP depended on did not function properly on newer versions of Windows, and the program had trouble printing bar codes on some printers. For these reasons, it was decided to redesign the ILL ASAP so that it would work well in a Web-based environment. As a result of the new design, which relies heavily on XML, ILL ASAP is more useful, easier to modify, and more reliable than its telnet-based predecessor.

PROJECT GOALS AND JUSTIFICATION

The goals of revising ILL ASAP were to automatically:

- identify whether a requested item exists in the catalog,
- record the location, call number, and availability of found items,
- identify the preferred means of sending the request (i.e., Ariel, fax, mail),
- keep track of borrowing agreements and billing arrangements, and
- generate forms that facilitate processing and that contain all information necessary to fill requests.

Also, it was hoped that the new version would be:

- easy to modify by staff with modest technical skills using any word processor,
- useful to other libraries, especially those in the Orbis consortium of which OSU is a member, and
- less prone to technical difficulties than the earlier version.

From an organizational point of view, it is risky for large institutions such as OSU to depend on locally developed applications based on technologies likely to become obsolete or to require highly specialized technical skills. XML technologies allow easy generation, retrieval, and manipulation of structured data stored in human-readable text files. Moreover, XML-based applications are relatively easy to modify to accommodate evolving needs, and XML support is rapidly growing for all major platforms.

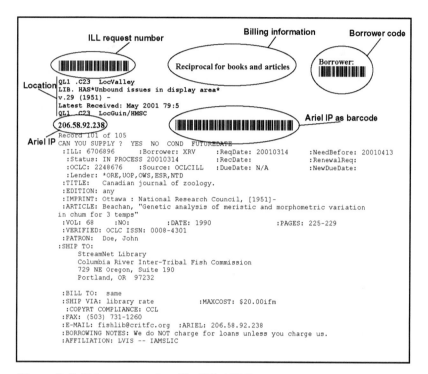

Figure 3–1. ILL request printed by ILL ASAP

PROJECT DESCRIPTION

Overview

ILL ASAP is an XML-based application that locates interlibrary loan requests downloaded from OCLC's ILL MicroEnhancer in OSU's Innovative Interfaces catalog. It then prints request forms containing availability and location information in call number order complete with bar codes representing the ILL request number, Ariel IP, and three-letter borrower code for quick processing. If transmitting requests via Ariel or fax is not possible, the program generates shipping labels. Billing information is also printed when appropriate. Figure 3–1 shows a typical request after it has been printed.

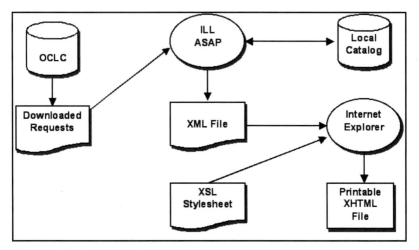

Figure 3–2. *ILL ASAP Processing*

Technical Details

ILL ASAP is a Visual Basic script that creates an XML file based on information extracted from a plain-text request file and the local catalog. Formatting, rendering, and printing of requests are handled by Internet Explorer's XSL support. When ILL ASAP is launched, it performs a series of tasks. First, it extracts useful information such as electronic and postal addresses of the borrower, control number, and borrower code from the interlibrary loan request file. It then searches for the requested items in the local catalog in public mode where it obtains location and availability information. Next, it creates an XML file containing information from the original request and the catalog. After the last request is searched, the XML file is sorted, formatted, and converted to XHTML using an XSL style sheet. Finally, the requests are printed. Figure 3–2 illustrates this process.

Why Use XSL?

One question that has been asked is why ILL ASAP creates an XML file that it immediately converts to XHTML. In other words, why doesn't ILL ASAP simply generate an XHTML file? The answer is that accomplishing what ILL ASAP does without XML would dramatically increase the complexity of the program while decreasing its flexibility. The selection and placement of fields on the printed page as well as the order in which requests are printed depend on the borrower's preferred mechanism for receiving requests, the relationship the borrowing institution has with Oregon State University, and the physical location of the item. It is possible to write programs to accomplish this in just about any language, but it is much easier and faster to use a single-page XSL style sheet to determine what prints where. Besides, making changes to the program without using XML is difficult and requires special programming skills.

XSL style sheets can perform many important tasks and can be modified by staff with modest technical skills. As a result, customizing the output to meet local needs is very easy. For example, the style sheet instruction:

```
<xsl:for-each order-by="+ callnum" select="requests/record">
```

sorts the requests in call number order. To sort requests on a different field, all that needs to be done is to change the contents of the "order-by" attribute. Likewise, positioning and formatting of special priority codes, shipping labels, or bar codes to facilitate processing is simply a matter of placing a tag such as:

```
<xsl:value-of select="shipto"/>
```

in an XHTML table within the style sheet. In addition to selecting and formatting information, XSL style sheets can make simple decisions. For instance, it is desirable for OSU to bill libraries for requested materials when there is no reciprocal lending arrangement with OSU. On the other hand, OSU should not send bills to lending partners. ILL ASAP automatically generates billing information only when no priority code containing information about the borrower is present. This is accomplished with a few simple lines:

```
<xsl:choose>
    <xsl:when test="priority">
```

```
<xsl:value-of select="priority"/>
  </xsl:when>
  <xsl:otherwise>
    <br/> Charge:_____
    <br/>Remit with copy to:
    <br/>Oregon State University
    <br/>Business affairs
    <br/>PO Box 1086
    <br/>Corvallis, OR 97339-1086
    <p/>FEIN #93-600-1786W
    <br/>Invoice#: LIBILL
  </xsl:otherwise>
</xsl:choose>
```

PROBLEMS AND CHALLENGES, SUCCESSES AND FAILURES

ILL ASAP accomplishes most of its design goals. It extracts accurate location and availability information associated with requested items, it presents certain critical information in a manner to facilitate processing (e.g., bar codes are generated for numeric Ariel IP addresses so that there is no need to type them, information about lending agreements with the borrower are printed in bold type at the top of the page, etc.), and the program has proven very easy to modify. For instance, it took less than five minutes to modify the program so that shipping labels would be generated automatically if the request could not be electronically transmitted, even though no thought had been given to shipping labels when the program was originally designed. Likewise, it took just a few minutes to accommodate a request to print the fax number in bold type at the top of the page when no Ariel address could be located.

The main area in which ILL ASAP has not fully realized its goals is portability. Because ILL ASAP searches the catalog in a public mode, it sees the same HTML as patrons do. As a result, about half of the libraries that try to implement ILL ASAP need to modify it to work with their catalogs. Fortunately, in most cases, these modifications are relatively minor. Having said that, several challenges emerged during the revision process. These challenges made a significant impact on the design of ILL ASAP and are described below.

Limited XML Support

XSL consists of three components: eXtensible Stylesheet Language Transformations (XSLT), XML Path language (XPath), and eXtensible Stylesheet Language Formatting Objects (XSL-FO). In a nutshell, XSLT is a language that transforms one kind of XML document into another, XPath is used by XSLT to select parts of a document and perform calculations and manipulations on data, and XSL-FO determines how elements will be rendered on the screen or on paper. The World Wide Web consortium approved the XSLT and XPath recommendations in November 1999, but had not yet approved the XSL-FO recommendation at the time of this writing.

When ILL ASAP was designed, Internet Explorer did not support a number of XPath expressions and functions necessary to perform certain selections and calculations within XSL style sheets. As a result, tasks that theoretically should have been handled by the style sheet either had to be written differently or were handed to a Visual Basic script. Another difficulty was that because XSL-FO had not been approved and was not supported by Internet Explorer, it was necessary to convert the requests to XHTML and use trial and error to format the requests in a manner that printed as desired.

XML support in the online catalog also created challenges. OSU's Innovative Interfaces system can output XML, but the bibliographic XML records do not contain control numbers of attached item and check-in records. Item records indicate whether a book is checked out or lost as well as the locations of individual copies, and the check-in records contain serials holdings summaries, so ILL ASAP needs to be able to examine data from multiple record types simultaneously. As a result, it was impractical to rely on the catalog's XML output functions. For this reason, ILL ASAP extracts information from the catalog by parsing HTML screens in public mode rather than retrieving data in XML. Fortunately, the text parsing routine used by

ILL ASAP works in most Innovative Interfaces systems with little or no modification.

Inherent Limitations of XML Technologies

Of the three XSL components listed above, XSLT is most central to the functionality of ILL ASAP. XSLT is extremely useful for simple selection and manipulation tasks, but it is not intended as a general-purpose XML transformation language. Rather, it exists primarily to perform manipulations required in the context of XSL style sheets. As a practical matter, this means that only string data can be output, and there is only a handful of basic tools available to select, manipulate, and present information. Moreover, XSLT is designed in such a way that it is impossible to change the value of a variable, use assignment operators, or perform tasks in any particular order. In short, XSLT cannot perform many basic functions taken for granted by most programmers.

These problems are not bugs or the result of functionality that has yet to be added, they are inherent to the thinking behind XSL. XSL is designed so that instructions can be executed in any order. The practical benefit of this design is that it allows different parts of a style sheet to be processed independently; this is known as progressive rendering. Progressive rendering allows small changes to be made to large documents in real time without any need to recalculate the whole document. Such a capability is clearly useful in a number of applications, such as creating interactive traffic maps or large charts containing live financial data. The drawback of this design is that assignment operations such as "x = x + 5" and "x = x/2" cannot be allowed because the final result depends on the order in which instructions are executed.

It is possible to circumvent some of the limitations of XSL through the use of creative programming techniques, but in many cases the only way to meet the need at hand is to perform functions in some other environment. For example, the XPath specification that describes how data is selected can only perform relatively primitive operations based on the names or contents of tags and attributes. As a result, there is no easy way to identify an untagged IP address or fax number within a request—these functions must be handled outside the style sheet.

PLANS

Interlibrary loan involves the transmission of copyrighted material, so rights management and statistical functions need to be built into any automated interlibrary loan software. Because OSU plans to purchase ILLiad resource sharing software to manage copyright compliance and generate statistics, the next version of ILL ASAP will be designed to work directly with ILLiad.

Innovative Interfaces plans to improve XML support, so ILL ASAP will be modified to work exclusively with XML once the control numbers of attached item and check-in records are included in bibliographic XML records. When this enhancement is made, the program should work reliably on all Innovative Interfaces systems. On a related note, only minor modifications to the program will be necessary to make it work with non-Innovative systems, so long as they allow retrieval of XML bibliographic, item, and check-in records from Web-based queries.

TIPS AND ADVICE (LESSONS LEARNED)

XML is very useful for presenting relatively small amounts of structured data such as reformatting interlibrary loan requests, but it is not an appropriate tool for many library applications. Processing XML is both memory and CPU intensive, and current XSLT processors are very slow. The reason for this is that XSLT processors must store all data in memory while transformations are performed because the processor must know the full structure of the document in order to apply templates. In addition, the amount of memory consumed by the transformations can be many times the size of the original document. Consequently, XSLT is not an appropriate technology for transforming documents on the fly, except when the document size is relatively small or relatively few documents need to be processed.

Anyone who is not intimidated by Cascading Style Sheets will not have much difficulty creating XSL style sheets that manipulate and present XML data. However, implementing XML-based projects will require a considerable amount of trial and error until the technology matures. A growing number of server-side packages can be installed to transform XML, but installing the packages is a task best left to those with some systems administration experience. On the other hand, relying on browser support of XML is impractical except when the control over the users' software is possible. In short, there are still significant technical issues associated with using XML, and projects need to be designed to accommodate the inherent limitations of XML technologies and the tools that are currently available.

IMPLICATIONS

Those who are interested in implementing XML for production work in libraries should examine their needs carefully before embarking on a project. First of all, is XML the best technology for the task at hand? XML is extremely useful for integrating, arranging, and manipulating data, but many common applications also perform these tasks. Unless XML is needed for a specific purpose, it may be an unnecessary extra step. On a similar note, XML is not an appropriate solution in situations in which the normal tool of choice would be a database. XML applications are slow and resource intensive, so it is not feasible from a technical point of view to use XSL to query large XML documents the way that SQL is used to query databases.

At the time of this writing, it was relatively difficult to find Web-based tutorials that are useful for implementing XML in a library setting. Part of the problem is that the technology is still new: more time needs to pass because many people who might normally write tutorials are still learning how to exploit XML for their own purposes. However, the greater barrier to implementation is determining what librarians want to accomplish with it. The power of XML is that its simplicity, flexibility, and extensibility make data easy to work with. However, if data can already be used as desired, no additional benefit will be gained by converting documents or records to XML. On the other hand, XML makes it possible to integrate services and resources in ways that would have been impossible just a few years ago. By spending some time to become familiar with the capabilities and limitations of XML, librarians will discover a multitude of ways to improve services and processes within their institutions.

CONTACT

Kyle Banerjee
Oregon State Library
260 Winter Street NE
Salem, OR 97331-0640
(503) 378-4243 x260
kyle.banerjee@state.or.us

LINKS AND RESOURCES

ILL ASAP Home Page
www.onid.orst.edu/~reeset/illasap/
Description of ILL ASAP, screen shots, and troubleshooting advice. The program can be downloaded for free.

XSL Description, Links to Tutorials, and More
www.w3.org/Style/XSL/
A gateway to information for people of all skill levels. Beginners should see the "Tutorials" section.

XSLT FAQ
www.dpawson.co.uk/xsl/sect2/sect21.html
An excellent collection of questions about XSLT, ranging from what it's good for to how it can be used to accomplish a wide variety of specific tasks. A valuable resource for people who already have a basic understanding of XSLT.

Application III

USING XML FOR CATALOGING & INDEXING

IN LIBRARIES

This section focuses on some of the most practical and timesaving of XML's applications: improved searching capabilites for cataloging and indexing.

CHAPTER 4

An archival finding aid is used by archivists to catalog and index archival collections. In Chapter 4, "Harnessing Oracle and XT for Finding Aid Dissemination and Search," Leslie Myrick explains how NYU is using Oracle and XT to make archival finding aids browsable, searchable, and far more practical.

CHAPTER 5

In Chapter 5, "Creating a Unified E-Government Portal Using XML," Sokvitne and Lavelle describe an innovative project by the State Library of Tasmania in which they used XML to stitch together access to a variety of government services into one easy-to-use portal. In doing so, they exhibit the best traditions of librarianship in using the most effective technologies at hand (in this case, XML) to organize and provide access to information for a particular clientele. This project illustrates that in the digital age, cataloging continues to be an effective and important activity, and that XML can form the foundation of descriptive systems just as MARC has for library catalogs.

CHAPTER 6

Chapter 6, "Expediting the Work of the Indexer with XML," is a demonstration of how indexes can be created by extracting specific terms from an XML-encoded document using software. Walter Lewis, Gail Richardson, and Geoff Cannon show that as libraries increasingly become involved with online publishing (see the *Building Collections* section), techniques such as this will become essential.

4

Harnessing Oracle and XT for Finding Aid Dissemination and Search

Leslie Myrick
New York University

BACKGROUND

Under the financial auspices of the Andrew W. Mellon Foundation and the technical auspices of the NYU Digital Library Team, two archival divisions of the New York Historical Society and three Special Collections archives at NYU are using a creative tool set to build an infrastructure for the production and dissemination of EAD-encoded finding aids marked up in XML. This project has to some extent entailed the conversion from legacy SGML to v.1 EAD XML-compliant documents; in other cases, XML documents have been produced through the ineffably onerous method of copying and pasting from Word documents into a WordPerfect template. These XML-encoded finding aids are then transformed either statically or dynamically into HTML using James Clark's XT transformation engine (although we are considering a move to Saxon or Xalan) and served up on an Apache Web server (see Figure 4–1). The final component is cross-collection search, which has been happily realized using Oracle interMedia Text. XT comes in again as the transformation engine behind the dynamic delivery of HTML from the XML original using a style sheet that incorporates a

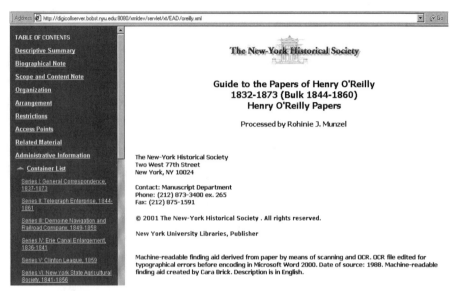

The New-York Historical Society

Guide to the Papers of Henry O'Reilly
1832-1873 (Bulk 1844-1860)
Henry O'Reilly Papers

Processed by Rohinie J. Munzel

The New-York Historical Society
Two West 77th Street
New York, NY 10024

Contact: Manuscript Department
Phone: (212) 873-3400 ex. 265
Fax: (212) 875-1591

© 2001 The New-York Historical Society . All rights reserved.

New York University Libraries, Publisher

Machine-readable finding aid derived from paper by means of scanning and OCR. OCR file edited for
typographical errors before encoding in Microsoft Word 2000. Date of source: 1988. Machine-readable
finding aid created by Cara Brick. Description is in English.

Figure 4–1. *The HTML version of an XML-encoded finding aid*

keyword search/highlighting template, to allow for simple
intrafinding aid search. As the metaphor in my title might suggest, to ply Oracle and XT in the same application could be perceived as being at best an anomaly—a bit like yoking a Ferrari
to the old gray mare, perhaps. However, it has proven to be an
agreeable and productive team for breaking new ground in the
delivery and querying of XML-encoded finding aids over the
Web.

PROJECT GOALS AND JUSTIFICATION

The goals of this project are to facilitate and, wherever possible,
to automate the production, dissemination, and searching of
EAD-encoded finding aids marked up in XML in the archival
collections of the New York Historical Society and NYU libraries. Most of the now extant finding aids were originally marked
up in SGML in the 1990s, for viewing at selected library work-
stations equipped with a proprietary SGML viewer. During that
same period, as a response to some obvious problems inherent
in SGML production and dissemination, another experimental
batch of finding aids came to light as encoded in HTML. The

bulk of legacy conversion yet to be undertaken involves the electronification of paper-based finding aids languishing in proprietary formats such as Word and WP. Add to the mix yet another batch with "generic" Apex tagging, and a clear picture of the need for structure and systems emerges.

If no justification was necessary for the development of a more robust production and delivery system, justification was, however, forthcoming for the notion of a servlet-based deployment of dynamically delivered HTML versions using XT as the transformation engine. A couple of the more obvious workflow related benefits in using a servlet-based approach are the following:

1. the possibility of posting valid documents straight to the Web server without the intermediary of running the XT executable on the PC, and
2. the existence of a centralized XSLT style sheet that can be emended once and redeployed immediately, rather than disseminated to and downloaded by any number of processing archivists.

Possible drawbacks would be these:

1. the maintenance issues for a more complex system dependent on numerous applications and their servers/wrappers/containers, and
2. the (perceived?) implication that the XML is both the archival copy and the disseminated copy in its instantiation as HTML.

PROJECT DESCRIPTION

Finding Aid Conversion and Production

NYU's Digital Library Team jumped firmly onto the EAD/XML bandwagon on the eve of the millennium, adopting the EAD XML DTD along with the EAD Cookbook recipe and accompanying style sheet as a basis for XSLT conversion to HTML. We use WordPerfect 2000 as an editing tool, with an adaptation of the template provided by the Cookbook site for the bulk of

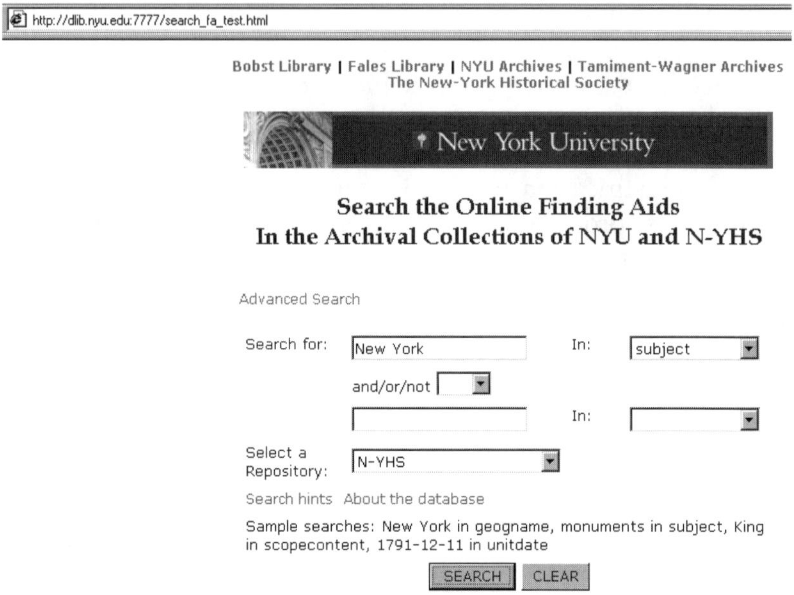

Figure 4–2. Search interface

our production. There was originally quite a bit of copy-and-paste activity and hand editing (as in the normalizing of dates), but that sort of task is being increasingly replaced by scripts.

Dissemination and Search

Present work flow dictates that once an XML-encoded finding aid validates it is converted to static HTML using the Windows-based XT executable. This static HTML frameset is ftp'ed to a staging server for vetting. The finalized HTML versions on the production server serve as an archive and are also pointed to by the results page generated from a query against the original XML-encoded version sitting in Oracle.

How they got into Oracle in the first place goes something like this: As finding aids become finalized they are loaded as CLOBs (character large objects), along with other bits of document metadata that will be displayed in the query results, into a table in Oracle 8i. The CLOB field is then indexed using interMedia Text to allow for cross-collection searching, either

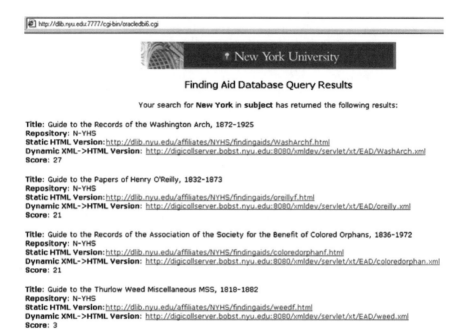

Figure 4–3. *Search results screen*

within specific tags or throughout the entire finding aid(s), as the user wishes.

From the present search interface (see Figure 4–2), the user can enter a simple or more complex search for a keyword or keywords either within tags or throughout entire documents. Once the search terms have been located in the indexes to the XML document, a pointer to the concomitant static HTML file is returned. So far so good, if all we want is to replicate the basic functionality of a Google or AltaVista. The finalized version will also contain a link pointing to the XML file itself that will be dynamically converted using XT or Saxon or Xalan, with the search term(s) passed as a parameter (see Figure 4–2). The extant prototype does almost as much, passing a single keyword with satisfactory results. What it lacks, of course, is the ability to match the complexity of the earlier search, which might have contained a Boolean or a theme-based query.

The features of Oracle interMedia Text search that we found compelling are many, but the possibility of Boolean and probabilistic search (relevance ranking) in a single query weighs most heavily. Also important to us (but remaining *in potentia* at this point) is the possibility of a multilingual search in the same query—a query combining English and a CJK term, for instance. Other mentionables are the usual array of advanced search functionalities: fully customizable stop lists and thesauri; stemming; fuzzy and soundex matching; and theme searching using an ABOUT operator. Speed is, of course, also an issue. Furthermore, interMedia Text proves to be omnivorous in that it can index entire documents whether within the database as CLOBs, on a file server as BFILE files, or as remote URLs (whose content it crawls). In the following section, I will outline the steps to setting up Oracle interMedia text search, a fairly straightforward process, for which there is ample documentation on the Oracle technet site and in a number of recently published Oracle manuals. Setup for the XT-XSLT search within a single finding aid will fall under another heading because it was in that architecture that most of the challenges and problems, successes and failures arose.

Oracle interMedia Text Search

The ingredients:

- Perl DBI as a database interface
- CGI.pm as a gateway and delivery script
- Oracle 8i with Oracle interMedia Text running on Solaris
- an Apache web server

Creating an Index:

The basic formula for creating an interMedia index is similar to the one for regular index creation in Oracle:

```
create index [name] on [tablename](column)
[params e.g. which stop list, which sectioner to use; space or storage params]
indextype is ctxsys.context.
```

or with the skeleton fleshed out:

```
CREATE INDEX findingaids_idx ON FINDINGAIDS(text)
[params]
INDEXTYPE IS ctxsys.context;
```

Selecting or Constructing a Section Group

The sectioner essentially winnows out the text from the metadata or section boundaries and adds the structural information it derives from this process to the index. The default is the null_section_group, which does not address tags in the document. There is also an auto_section_group that adds to the index any tag it comes upon, without the need for predefinition; a basic_section_group, which can be used for simple, well-formed XML; an html_section_group, which includes the basic HTML tagset; and an xml_section_group, which you must construct yourself by defining fields or zones.

To create a section group, enter a variation of the following command into SQLPlus:

```
ctx_ddl.create_section_group('findingaids','xml_section_group');
```

Define the Sections

There are three types of sections: Zone, Special, and Field. Zone and Special sections simply use start and end word offsets, while Field sections extract the contents of the fields and index them separately from other words in the document. The Field section, much speedier but less flexible than the others, is that which I am intimately familiar with, so I will use it as my example below.

Sections have three attributes: tag, name, and type. To add a field for the scopecontent element in an EAD-encoded finding aid, type into SQLPlus:

```
ctx_ddl.add_field_section('scopecontent', 'scope and content', 'tag');
```

Attributes can also be added to the xml_section_group. If, for instance, you wish to allow for search specifically on inclusive dates in a finding aid, the command for adding an attribute section would be:

```
ctx_ddl.add_attr_section('findingaids','inclusivedate','inclusive@unitdate');
```

Search

The SQL statement needed to query documents containing the words "New York" in proximity to "Arch" in the scopecontent field of a finding aid and to return a relevancy score is as follows:

```
SELECT score(1), repository, eadid, url
FROM FINDINGAIDS
WHERE CONTAINS (text,
'New York NEAR Arch WITHIN scopecontent' > 0)
ORDER BY score(1) DESC;
```

The WITHIN operator can be combined with standard SQL in the WHERE clause. For instance, to specify a certain collection in which to search:

```
SELECT score(1), repository, eadid, url
FROM FINDINGAIDS
WHERE repository = 'NYHS' AND CONTAINS (text, 'New York NEAR Arch WITHIN
scopecontent' > 0) ORDER BY score(1) DESC;
```

PROBLEMS AND CHALLENGES, SUCCESSES AND FAILURES

The most obvious unresolved problem lies in the fact that the intrafinding aid search mechanism, using XT and an XSLT style sheet match/highlight template, cannot fully replicate the complexity of the previous Oracle search. Here is where the Ferrari/ old gray mare pairing becomes worrisome. Further development that takes full advantage of the Oracle XDK/Servlet and Java tool set is forthcoming and will most likely lead to a more equitable pairing.

To have come this far with the EAD Cookbook style sheet/ XT combination has, however, involved some interesting challenges, which I will outline below.

The Dynamic Intra-Document Search Prototype Using XT and James Clark's Servlet

The ingredients:

- a valid XML EAD document
- a heavily reworked version of eadcbs3.xsl
- a .css style sheet to prettify the output
- the XT transformation engine
- the Tomcat servlet engine
- an Apache Web server

The EAD Cookbook style sheet that we inherited had to be rewritten to dynamically split the XML document into four parts to plug into the HTML frameset. As far as I know, this is most easily undertaken using XT as a processor; I know from another project that Xalan within the larger Cocoon framework can also do this. I haven't yet wrestled Saxon into pulling it off, although I suspect it can be done.

The style sheet's treatment of the entire <dsc> section also underwent a sea change to rely more on walking the tree and conditional processing of the nodes for the production of <c01>s and <c02>s. For the most part, this was necessary to allow for varying formats (a combination of box and folder, bound volume, and/or reel) within the same collection.

The search/highlighting template that has been incorporated into the style sheet is a basic recursive substring match template adapted from the DynaXML style sheet written by Kirk Hastings (and available on his Web site cited below), but more thoroughly applied throughout. The template searches for the keyword as a substring, applies highlighting to it (in this case, red font and font amplification by one size), and delivers the text to the front and rear of the keyword substring untouched. This template is called with any <xsl:apply-templates/> element where search is desired in that template match.

The Style Sheet

The initial impulse to rewrite eadcbs3.xsl arose from a desire to be able to deliver frame-based finding aids dynamically us-

ing XT, my R&D transformation engine of choice at the time of
the idea's inception. It was equally driven by the intractability
of the present Cookbook style sheet versions in rendering truly
mixed collections, i.e., those containing more than just box and
folder within the same collection, interspersed with, say, reels
or bound volumes. Both of these issues were well addressed by
rewriting the <dsc> element and its descendents.

Character Entity References

A rather nagging problem has been the strange treatment of
character entities in the WordPerfect XML editor, a problem that
is compounded by more of the same in the process of static
HTML conversion using XT. Saxon's treatment seems to be the
most promising on this front, and we may shift to Instant Saxon
for any static production of HTML for archival use and eventually for dissemination if it can be successfully integrated into
the servlet environment.

Oracle Challenges

The Oracle end of the equation was the less problematic, but
there were a few quirks along the way. For instance, it took more
than one try to pull off inserting CLOBs into Oracle from the
command line in SQL*LOADER. An outstanding project is to
create a batch loading .sql script using Perl DBI to automate and
speed up this process altogether.

Under the category of curiosities, there are the "malformed
UTF-8" error messages thrown by the EAD DTD files when
Oracle tries to validate a finding aid. For this reason the pointer
to the DTD has been suppressed in the (already validated) XML
version that is loaded into the Oracle table. There were similar
problems in this area with Xalan as well.

According to the literature, what interMedia text search in
its 8i incarnation lacks in XPATH axis-traversing and pattern-
matching precision it seems to be recouping in 9i, which also
touts a new XMLtype native datatype that uses native search
mechanisms.

PLANS

In the ongoing debate on the trade-off between ease and speed (Perl) vs. robustness (Java), the latter may well win out. I'm quite certain that I will very soon find myself rewriting the search engine in Java using a JDBC interface, with Servlet delivery of the HTML, rather than in Perl DBI and CGI.pm.

The most obvious desideratum is to synchronize the two searches by passing the entire Oracle query to the XSLT conversion, so that the complete query will be replicated with the terms highlighted in the dynamically generated HTML. This may involve replicating more complex searches in a new style sheet using the improved XPATH functionality in the latest Oracle avatar.

Another improvement would be to extract the metadata programmatically from the XML document itself, probably using the XML SQL utility; this would entail analyzing (at least the pre-<dsc> matter of) an XML document into fields and loading it into a relational table structure. Then extracts such as abstracts or scope and content notes could be pulled out and delivered in the results pages without having been manually entered into table fields.

TIPS AND ADVICE (LESSONS LEARNED)

First and foremost, dare to be square.

When I sent the URL for my XT-based search to a friend, the reply he quickly fired back was "No XT! R.I.P." But until this application is superceded (in the near future), I see it as a viable proof-of-concept solution *ex nihilo*.

We jumped into Oracle development with both feet the minute the Digital Library Team won its share in the campus site-license. InterMedia Text search was a fast, easily implemented solution to cross database search—it took about two days to put it in place. The question for me then, was how to integrate that bleeding-edge implementation with concurrent development of an XSLT style sheet using XT that would dynamically deliver our individual finding aids, especially once I had integrated Kirk's search/highlight template into the mix.

The solution may finally send the old gray mare out to pasture, but until I can write my own processor, or beat Oracle's into submission, this combination offers a search package that clearly beats nothing.

IMPLICATIONS

As it stands, this sort of XSLT-based transformation that passes a search term to the style sheet to produce a refreshed version of the document with the search term highlighted validates the use of dynamically generated HTML.

It also demonstrates to some extent how Oracle can be made to play agreeably with open-source tools such as Perl, CGI.pm, and XT.

CONTACTS

Leslie Myrick
Digital Library Programmer/Analyst
NYU Libraries
70 Washington Square South
New York, NY 10012
leslie.myrick@nyu.edu

LINKS AND RESOURCES

The Digital Library Team homepage at NYU
www.nyu.edu/library/bobst/collections/digilib/digicollhome.html
What we're up to here at NYU.

The NYU EAD Production Guide
www.nyu.edu/library/bobst/collections/findingaids/ead/
Take our style sheets. Please. Everything you need (but warm bodies) to process EAD in WordPerfect.

NYU Archival Finding Aids Search
dlib.nyu.edu:7777/search_fa.html
The search interface to the NYU finding aids.

Oracle Text (in its new incarnation with 9i)
otn.oracle.com/products/text/content.html
Learn more about Oracle full-text search.

Searching XML Data with Oracle Text (9i)
download-east.oracle.com/otndoc/oracle9i/901_doc/
appdev.901/a88894/adx08txt.htm
Another article on the full-text search capabilities of Oracle Text.

The EAD Cookbook
www.iath.virginia.edu/ead/cookbookhelp.html
Tools galore for setting up a workflow for EAD production.

Kirk Hasting's DynaXML site
bodoni.village.virginia.edu:2020/servlet/DefaultApplyXSL/
documentation/dynaXML.xml?xslURL=/documentation/xsl/
dynaxml.xsl
An exciting prototype for replicating Dynaweb-like text delivery and search using XSLT.

5

Creating a Unified
E-Government Portal Using XML

Lloyd Sokvitne and Jan Lavelle
State Library of Tasmania

BACKGROUND

Service Tasmania is the name of a project established by the Tasmanian State Government in 1997 to provide a simple and integrated way for the Tasmanian community to access government services. To this end, government services in Tasmania have been progressively unified through the provision of single shop fronts transacting a variety of government services, through simplified and unified telephone services, and most recently through the provision of a single government services portal on the Internet.

The State Library of Tasmania was contracted by the state government of Tasmania to develop and manage the *Service* Tasmania Web portal. In part this was recognition of the role performed by the State Library in the development and maintenance of *Tasmania Online* (www.tas.gov.au), a comprehensive index to all Tasmanian content on the Web. During 1999-2000 the State Library developed the software and functionality behind the Web site, and *Service* Tasmania Online (www.service.tas.gov.au) went live in May 2000.

The resultant *Service* Tasmania Online site is a government services portal that has been developed and is maintained by

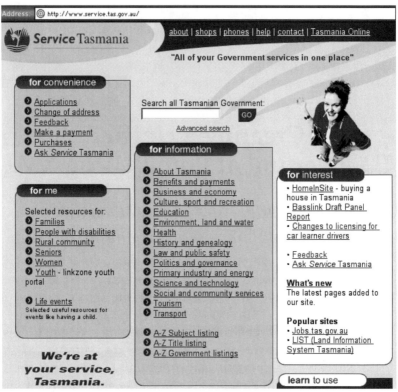

Figure 5–1. *Service Tasmania Online homepage*

professional librarians. As such, it uses indexing and retrieval principles and a customer-focus based on expertise and values inherited from the librarianship profession. The result is a new and innovative approach to Web discovery, based on an XML data store, that provides the end user with integrated access to resources from state, federal, and municipal governments.

Users of *Service* Tasmania Online can search for government information and services by a variety of customer-focused approaches and interlinked access points, on a Web site that is fast to load and straightforward to use, with simple icons and accurate descriptions to identify government resources and their originating jurisdiction. *Service* Tasmania Online also offers a range of online bill payment services for the state government and some local governments, application forms, and inquiry, help, and feedback facilities.

PROJECT GOALS AND JUSTIFICATION

The key objective of the *Service* Tasmania Online Web site is to enable members to the Tasmanian community to locate government services and information without any prior knowledge as to which level of government or which department/agency provides the information or service they seek, and without knowing the format of the resource that best meets their need. This means that the site must include and integrate a variety of government resources from all three tiers of government (municipal, state, and federal).

Accessibility needs dictated that the retrieval and display system should meet the widest possible range of user requirements within the community, and be fast and easy to deliver to a variety of platforms and over a range of network capacities. The software and Web delivery system must be inherently flexible over time, and technologically independent, yet meet a limited budget. Finally, the Web site should be based on a data management system that allows the site to be generated from that data automatically, thereby reducing site and HTML page maintenance.

The State Library is part of the Department of Education, and most computer applications are managed by a central technology group. The range of applications used within the department include a major library information management system (GEAC), large financial and administration software packages, and a wide range of desktop applications (largely based on Microsoft products). The department has some experience in XML and had recently developed an XML-based application that allowed teachers to create descriptions of learning resources that are then available though a single education-orientated Web site called *Discover*. This wide range of expertise allowed the State Library to review a large number of possible options in its development of *Service* Tasmania Online while still remaining within an area that matched internal skills and capabilities.

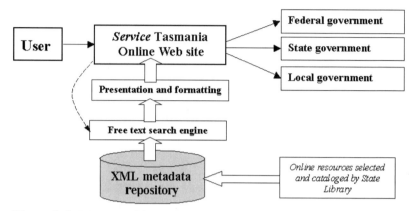

Figure 5–2. *Diagram of Service Tasmania online*

PROJECT DESCRIPTION

The software developed for *Service* Tasmania Online is called the Resource Discovery Service (RDS). This system is based on a central metadata repository that uses XML files to contain descriptions (metadata) about the government resources that are to be made available on the Web site. The XML files are indexed by using Microsoft's Site Server search engine software. Most options and links on the Web site are disguised search statements that interrogate this search engine and reformat the results according to presentation and data rules.

A system based on a data repository that would automatically generate site content required controlled and accurate resource descriptions (metadata). This metadata had to be highly specific, yet consistent in terms of access points, vocabularies, and subject terms. This controlled and structured metadata also had to be simple to enter, easy to index, and flexible in terms of output and reuse possibilities. For these reasons, we decided to build an XML system from scratch rather than using traditional library and MARC-based systems.

Many government portals are based on systems that harvest remote metadata, but this approach was rejected because it limited content to only those resources for which metadata already existed. It also relied on local data standards for metadata creation that were often very poor.

A centrally created metadata repository in turn allowed us to create high-quality metadata and to include online resources irrespective of their native format's ability to house or make metadata descriptions available to external software (e.g., PDF files, images, etc.).

Another significant benefit from a central repository model was the capacity to specifically select resources across government that should be included on the Web portal. This met our overall objective to provide accurate and directed retrieval, rather than simply including all possible resources just because they were located within government. We estimated that of the 100,000+ electronic resources available across government, users of the entry portal needed to be referred to less than 10 percent of those resources. These resources were those that were the most relevant to the general community, were in high demand, were intrinsically difficult to locate, or were themselves entry points into internal indexes and retrieval facilities that did not need duplication on the portal site.

The *Service* Tasmania Online central metadata repository comprises metadata stored as XML files, with one XML file per resource. The XML files are created and edited using Web-based input screens that include a large of number of controlled vocabulary lists and data validation processes to ensure that the information is accurate and consistent. Librarians from the State Library of Tasmania carry out the professional task of indexing resources to ensure that the metadata is consistent and accurate.

XML was used as the basis for this metadata repository because it allowed the Library to develop an internal data structure that was specific for *Service* Tasmania Online and the needs of the Web site. The metadata within the XML files is used to provide all navigation and content on the Web site. This reduces the workload associated with site presentation maintenance and management. It also means that changes to retrieval requirements or the provision of new options to meet user needs can be provided by simply modifying the data or adding new query statements, rather than by making major changes to the Web site presentation software itself.

The data schema and structure of the XML records were designed to be able to produce Dublin Core and Australian Government Locator Service output. The actual schema is designed with much greater internal granularity than Dublin Core, and it reflects a need to structure the data in ways that can deliver a wider range of retrieval options as well as augment site maintenance and management processes.

Sample record:

```
<XML>
  <RDS>
    <ID>00000182</ID>
    <ResourceType>Web Page</ResourceType>
    <CreatedBy>Jan Lavelle</CreatedBy>
    <CreatedOn>2001-05-01T00:00:00</CreatedOn>
    <DisplayTitle>Seniors Card</DisplayTitle>
    <URL>http://www.dhhs.tas.gov.au/seniors/card/</URL>
    <DisplayDateStart>2000-09-22T00:00:00</DisplayDateStart>
    <ReviewDate>2001-03-21T00:00:00</ReviewDate>
    <LastModifiedOn>2001-09-07T08:18:34</LastModifiedOn>
    <LastModifiedBy>Michael French</LastModifiedBy>
    <URLStatus>Live</URLStatus>
    <URLStatusMessage>Ok</URLStatusMessage>
    <URLStatusDate>2002-01-24T22:15:45</URLStatusDate>
    <URLDateLastSighted>2002-01-24T22:15:45</URLDateLastSighted>
  </RDS>
  <AGLS>
    <Title>Seniors Card</Title>
    <Description>About the Seniors Card, making Tasmanians over 60 not in paid
employment eligible for a range of discounts and concessions. Links to printable ap-
plication form, update form and contacts (PDF files)</Description>
    <Identifier>
      <Value>http://www.dhhs.tas.gov.au/seniors/card/</Value>
    </Identifier>
    <Subject>
      <Value>Concessions</Value>
    </Subject>
    <Subject>
      <Value>Seniors</Value>
    </Subject>
    <Creator>Tasmania. Dept. of Health and Human Services</Creator>
    <Date>
      <Value>20010906</Value>
```

```
    </Date>
    <Publisher>Tasmania. Dept. of Health and Human Services</Publisher>
    <Type>
        <Value>text</Value>
    </Type>
    <Format>
        <Value>text/html</Value>
    </Format>
    <Language>en</Language>
    <Rights>http://www.tased.edu.au/webgov/codi.htm</Rights>
  </AGLS>
  <STO>
    <Task>Applications</Task>
    <Community>Seniors</Community>
    <OrganisationType>State government</OrganisationType>
    <Agency>Health and Human Services</Agency>
    <FullTopic>Social and community services \ Concessions \ Seniors card</
FullTopic>
  </STO>
</XML>
```

A search engine, Microsoft Site Server, is used to index the XML files in the metadata repository, and the Web site is delivered out of the search engine indexes. This methodology was chosen in order to take advantage of the high performance that a search engine could provide and that the Web site required. The search engine catalogs, set up to be able to index the data descriptions in XML correctly, act as a virtual database, providing the structure that would otherwise require a database approach. A system based on a database was rejected because of concerns over a database's ability to meet the high Web-oriented performance expectations of the portal wherein each page would be the result of multiple conjoined queries, the inherent inflexibility and high cost of functional alternations to a database over the long term, and the problems of data modeling involved with repeating metadata fields.

Although the use of XML files and search engine software was the relatively simple combination of two basic technologies, specific software developments were required to allow for the range of specific retrieval and display requirements of the site:

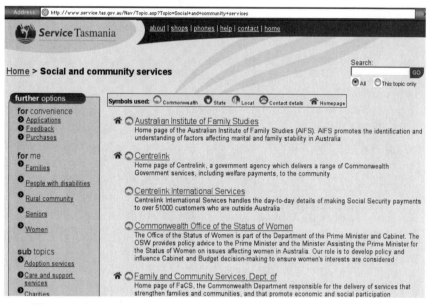

Figure 5–3. *Example of cross-linked options*

1. Multiple alternative retrieval options beyond subject access. It was recognized that there were needs in the community to access government resources in ways that extend beyond the basic topic or subject approach familiar to most libraries. For example, members of the community could potentially look for resources based on what they were trying to do or achieve. This is a task-based approach that includes options such as making a payment, applying for a service, etc. The community is also likely to search for content according to special or target audiences (e.g., youth, women, people with disabilities), key life events (having a baby, getting a driver's license), geographic relevance, the format of a resource, or other special characteristics (what's new, what's popular, documents out for public comment, etc.). The metadata had to store all of these potential access points, ensure there were controls for their assignment and use, and allow them to be presented on the Web site as required.

2. Retrieval options that are cross-linked. Software was developed that allowed end users to retain alternative access options even after choosing a top-level access strategy. Alternative access options are presented only when actual resources are available. For example, a user who chooses the topic "Social and

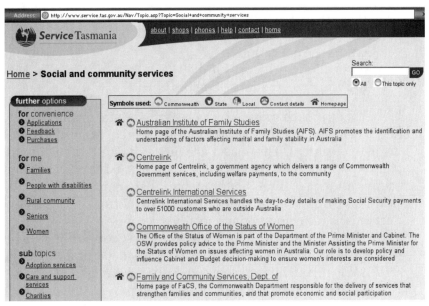

Figure 5–4. *Example of cross-linking to include target audience options*

community services" will receive a page with general social and community services resources. This page also offers a range of tasks that relate to social and community services (e.g., applications) as well as a range of target audiences for that topic.

If "Applications" were then subsequently chosen, the target audience option still appears on the results page (provided there are target audiences that apply to the conjoined query "Social and community services" and "Applications"). In the example shown in Figure 5–4, resources for seniors are still available.

This cross-linking is a type of post-coordinate indexing based on the principle that the access options are combined as choices made as the user moves through the site (rather than having all such choices predetermined). This means that the end user can successfully browse to find the application for a seniors discount card nine ways:

> Social and community services—Concessions—Seniors Card
> Social and community services—Seniors
> Social and community services—Applications
> Social and community services—Applications—Seniors

Social and community services—Seniors—Applications
Seniors—Concessions
Seniors—Applications
Applications—Seniors Card
Applications—Seniors—Seniors Card

This approach required special software to ensure that the alternative access options were only offered when there was available content. This was a challenge due to the huge number of permutations theoretically possible, and it was achieved through the use of in-memory tables that are created from the XML and that store all relevant combinations of facets as determined by the underlying metadata records.

3. Development of a Web-friendly browsable subject navigation hierarchy. A purpose-designed natural-language browsable hierarchy provides subject-based navigation through the Web site. This hierarchy is designed to provide the user with a small number of top-level terms, and to expand to only two sublevels. This approach is taken to ensure the user does not need to execute more than a few clicks to reach the required resource. The construction of the hierarchy was based on the range of content actually available in the government online environment and according to the principle that each level of the hierarchy should expand only when there are sufficient resources to require that expansion, and that levels should expand if there are too many results to browse easily (normally about 20 resources).

4. Provide free-text searching to both the metadata and the text on the described page. Free-text searching was seen as a necessary component of retrieval on the Web site, but ways were sought to provide better precision and lower recall. To do this, the software routines were developed to provide a free-text index to just the metadata within the XML records together with the free text on the particular Web page described by that metadata. This provided access to the quality terms in the metadata as well as the words that occur on the actual Web page. This type of free-text searching, which is the default offered on the homepage, proved to be very effective. It is still possible to access an expansive free-text option that indexes all the documents harvested across all the government servers. The free-text index is refreshed nightly.

5. **Context-sensitive free-text searching.** Software was developed that enabled free-text searches made within the site to assume a starting point based on the topic already chosen. The results from this type of free-text search are much more relevant to end users because they are limited to the subject context and environment where the search is made.

6. **Synonym augmentation in free-text searching.** When entering free-text terms, the user is unlikely to consider or include synonyms of those terms, and misspellings are common. A special synonym table has been created that is matched against the user-entered search terms before the search is executed. Additional synonyms and alternative spellings are then added to the search, unknown to the user. This approach, rather than term substitution, has been taken to allow the search to include the wider range of terms that could appear within the documents themselves. This also allows for the possibility that misspellings may actually occur in the content being searched. For example, the word *accommodation* is often misspelled in the online environment, and if only the correct spelling were used as a search term, relevant resources would be missed.

7. **Free-text indexing across hidden linked files.** Hidden free-text searching means that the software can link a number of resources within the metadata so that a free-text search can include those linked resources. For example, the entry page to an annual report made up of multiple single physical documents is used as the central link, but all the subsequent pages are also indexed. Free-text searches can then include all the content of the documents within the annual report without the need to provide metadata records for each document.

8. **Automatic URL verification and metadata update.** A specific program was developed to ensure that the metadata repository and the Web site reflected changes to the status of Web resources and that resources that no longer existed were excluded. This program removes a Web site from the results display when it can no longer be found, and adds it again should it reappear. The program has variable parameters that allow the site administrator to determine how many unsuccessful accesses

are required before that site is automatically removed from results lists.

**9. Web-based entry forms with a variety of controlled
vocabularies and validation routines.** A specific challenge was
enabling access within a Web-based data entry form to a large
hierarchical topic thesaurus with approximately 1,000 terms.
The solution required that the topic thesaurus was itself kept
as an XML file and indexed by the search engine. This was then
made available within the input form, and allowed use of a synonym table to assist the indexers when looking for appropriate
topics.

**10. Generating automated title, agency, and government
portfolio listings.** Alphabetical access to Web resources is available via title listings that are produced automatically from the
XML. An alphabetical listing of the homepages of government
departments by jurisdiction level is also available, as is an amal-
gamation of government department homepages arranged by
the minister responsible for those departments.

PROBLEMS AND CHALLENGES, SUCCESSES
AND FAILURES

Service Tasmania Online received two major national Australian
awards in 2001: the biennial Victorian Automated Libraries Association (VALA) award for innovation in library information
systems, and the silver award at the Australian 2001 Government Technology Productivity Awards.

A major outcome of the success of *Service* Tasmania Online
has been the recognition by state government that librarians
have an important role as information experts in the online
arena. The State Library of Tasmania is involved with many aspects of state government online information management,
including participation in strategic ICT planning processes
and the development of whole-of-government Web publishing
standards.

XML has proven be a powerful and flexible data storage
medium, and we have been able to use XML data as the basis
for other Web services. The State Library has been able to extract the data from MARC records in a library catalog and con-

vert them into XML files that can be used by our search engine and retrieval system. This has allowed the quick development of a powerful images Web site for the State Library that goes well beyond the capacity of traditional MARC-based systems. The XML record structure has also been used to develop a state-wide youth portal and an investment gateway.

One of the major issues that has emerged stems from the fact that many aspects of online Web retrieval require new approaches for which there is little established research or precedent. This has meant that we have had to take experimental approaches and accept that we must modify strategies if they do not produce desired results. There is also an ongoing overhead in monitoring and adapting processes to fit a new and developing environment. For example, our policies on determining which Web sites across government are the core sites needed by the community are constantly under scrutiny. We also continually review our browsable navigation hierarchy to ensure it continues to reflect available subject matter and that each level of a hierarchy is populated with the appropriate amount of resources.

An ongoing problem with the use of flat XML text files for data storage has been the difficulty of making data changes without the capabilities of a relational database. For example, if a creator name changes, that creator name has to be updated in each individual record. A scripting tool has been developed that allows batch changes to the XML data in selected records or directories, but this is not seen as an adequate long-term solution.

Software and programming problems have emerged, as would be expected from any new development. Our custom-written software has occasionally proven complex and difficult to debug as enhancements are added. We have also found that established enterprise software, search engines, Web server software, and so on can act unpredictably when pushed to the limit in terms of performance and enhanced functionality. Bugs found at these outer levels are often obscure and difficult to resolve with the software provider.

PLANS

Processes are currently under way to convert our state portal, *Tasmania Online*, to the same XML-based system used by *Service* Tasmania Online. *Tasmania Online* is a comprehensive index of all Tasmanian content on the Web, and includes commercial, community, and government Web sites. As such, *Tasmania Online* is a superset of the *Service* Tasmania Online XML data store.

An aspect of this process was the need to modify the software so that the same XML files can drive a wider variety of access options and presentation formats. Our initial software was based on the concept of a separate XML data store for each Web site, but we now recognize the need to use and share XML data and to drive multiple Web sites from the same records.

We are also developing software to deliver results from our search engine in XML format and to deliver those results via HTTP/SOAP to requesting applications. These applications could then use XSL to format the results to suit their own presentation and usage requirements. Such an approach will make our system much more neutral and flexible in its ability to provide data indexing and retrieval services for other Web sites.

Another development currently under way is the addition of the capacity to send queries to X500/LDAP systems based on information contained within the XML metadata records. This will allow our Web site to include accurate and current government phone numbers in relevant search results.

TIPS AND ADVICE (LESSONS LEARNED)

Our major advice to others would be to build systems that recognize that the most important component of any retrieval system is the underlying data. This data should be maintained as consistently and accurately as possible, and should be independent of the systems that deliver the final service to the client. XML has proven to be an ideal format, both neutral and flexible. By using XML, we have been able to enhance and change retrieval outputs by changing the underlying data, rather than by rewriting the software.

We have also found it to be beneficial to use standard applications whenever possible and to write custom components only when unavoidable. This allows the substitution of individual applications as alternatives become available or necessary. But it should also be noted that even proprietary software can have bugs or inconsistencies that produce unforseen results. Testing regimes should always cover the full end-to-end process.

Finally, we would add that it is not necessary to develop all the anticipated functional requirements for the first or early production phases of a site. It has been our experience that of the range of possible requirements, only a small set of core requirements is actually needed to operate a successful Web site. By focusing only on core requirements, sites can be available much sooner, with additional functionality added later or changed as new needs emerge. We have found it is better to be operational early rather than trying to have everything possible ready. Many of the things we put off at the start for subsequent phases have since been superseded or proven unnecessary.

IMPLICATIONS

Experience in Tasmania has shown that libraries have the skills and expertise to develop metadata management and information retrieval systems that specifically meet the needs of modern electronic resource discovery. Information providers are prepared and often willing to accept the expertise that librarianship offers in this arena. The challenge for libraries is to move beyond traditional MARC or cataloging-based approaches and to adapt new technologies to meet user needs.

The Resource Discovery Service as developed by the State Library of Tasmania has demonstrated the ability of XML to manage discovery data in sufficient granularity and with an inherent structure that permits flexible and effective retrieval. The strength of XML has been that it has allowed the development of retrieval approaches outside of the book-orientated limitations inherent in the MARC structure. The neutrality of XML also allows a discovery service to interact with the online environment through harvesting and free-text indexing services across different providers without the overhead and complexity of Z39.50 query interfaces and compliant MARC data structures.

CONTACTS

Lloyd Sokvitne
int + 61 + 3 + 6233 7632
lloyd.sokvitne@education.tas.gov.au

Jan Lavelle
jan.Lavelle@education.tas.gov.au

LINKS AND RESOURCES

Service **Tasmania Online**
www.service.tas.gov.au
The first State Library of Tasmania Web site based on the XML-based Resource Discovery System.

Tasmania Online
www.tas.gov.au
A comprehensive index to Tasmanian content on the Web that now utilizes the XML-based Resource Discovery System.

Sites developed by the State Library of Tasmania based on the XML-based RDS application:
Discover, discover.tased.edu.au
LinkZone Youth Portal, www.linkzone.com.au
State Library of Tasmania Images Service, images.statelibrary. tas.gov.au/
Tasmanian Infrastructure and Resource Information Service, www.iris.tas.gov.au

Awards won by the Government Portal service developed by the State Library:

Victorian Association for Library Automation, www.service. tas.gov.au/stabout/award_vala.htm

National Government Technology Productivity Award,
www.service.tas.gov.au/stabout/award_tech.htm

About *Service* Tasmania Online
www.service.tas.gov.au/papers/index.htm
Policy and design issues affecting the development of an information architecture for a government resource discovery service.

6

Expediting the Work of the Indexer with XML

Walter Lewis, Gail Richardson, and Geoff Cannon
Halton Hills Public Library

BACKGROUND

One of the measures of a good nonfiction title has long been the quality of its index. In an era when the entire contents of a book or a whole collection of volumes can be made full-text searchable, is the whole concept of indexing, especially by humans, hopelessly outdated?

It is perhaps a limitation of the human imagination that "names" are endlessly recycled in new contexts. A family of settlers moves into a region. The eldest son is named for his father; the eldest daughter for her mother. A community grows up around them and is named for the family. Various business ventures are founded and named, in part, for the community: mills, ships, institutions of learning, even a library. When the electronic version of the community's history is released, an ordinary full-text search may have a very high level of recall, returning hundreds of hits, but how do we narrow them to the references to the ship?

In traditional collections, we search first on a limited number of controlled-vocabulary subject headings in the library catalog or the journal indexes. A second level of search is possible at the level of the item, whose scope is largely within the purview of the publisher. With the electronic collection comes the promise of rapidly searching across an entire collection of materials. How can we improve the relevance of the results?

The answer within the individual document may still be the index. But is this approach reasonable for a large set of electronic documents? How can we balance the vast number of relevant terms in a given work with the limited time and funds available for human review of the index terms?

Our approach for XML documents was to automate the initial stages of markup, flag ambiguous terms, and then follow up with a review by someone familiar with the work.

PROJECT GOALS AND JUSTIFICATION

The project goals were simple:

- create electronic documents using a standardized markup scheme recognized in the digital library community
- enhance search and retrieval of elements within these documents by automating, as much as was reasonable, the identification of relevant index pointers

The Text Encoding Initiative (TEI) has specific advantages for these goals in that it facilitates a variety of levels of encoding, some of which exist merely to represent the original document and others that allow us to enhance the tagging with value-added editorial content. The TEI Lite standard includes a number of standard elements for indexing purposes: <index>, <rs>, and <name>. Available for use is an extended set of name tags that are not part of the base set (including <persName>, <placeName>, and <orgName>). We chose not to employ them, but doing so would require relatively little enhancement of the present tool set. The challenge was dealing with documents in which thousands of proper names appear. It was felt that it should be possible to automate proper name tagging in a way that normalizes (or regularizes, using the "reg" attribute) the references, still dependent on a human editor/indexer for review.

This may prove, as it has for us, to be of particular interest to those librarians, indexers, and catalogers trying to meet the need of genealogists and others using local history material. The ability to contextualize names and phrases into such basic categories as people, places, and things, will undoubtedly become an essential feature of full-text searching.

PROJECT DESCRIPTION

This approach led us to develop three small tools written in Perl to facilitate the markup. Each of them assumes that it is being supplied a valid TEI document and does its best to ensure that nothing is rendered invalid in the course of markup. As always, the possibility of operator-introduced error exists.

XMLAttributes

Perhaps the simplest of the tools, XMLAttributes, was built simply **to facilitate the addition of attributes to specific elements**. In order for the final indexes to be able to locate text, they require "ID" attributes for tags like paragraph, line group, illustrations, and the various division levels (<p>, <lg>, <figure>, and <div>). It was in our interest that they be sequential within any given element so that index terms could be presented in the same order as in the original document. With hundreds of such elements in some documents, hand-coding the IDs proved to be a lengthy and error-prone process, so we automated it.

We adapted this routine to add other attributes to all occurrences of the element. For example, in a number of documents, each <div1> element might well require a type="chapter" attribute. Again it is up to the operator to ensure that the attribute is named correctly, that it is valid across the occurrences, and that the value being assigned is also appropriate. The utility does force the user to supply a different file name for output so that a second, corrected pass can be made if necessary.

XMLNames.pl

The purpose of this utility is to check the document for strings that match a database table of naturally occurring names that may be relevant for indexing. Ambiguous strings can be flagged in the source dataset (we use "***") in ways that facilitate check-ing by a human indexer.

The process starts with a table defined as follows:

```
CREATE TABLE Names (
    NameID int,
    Reg char (100),
    Occurrence char (100),
    Type char (50),
    LengthofOcc int)
```

In nearly 9,000 strings, our longest occurrence was 53 and reg was 82. Because drive space is inexpensive these days, we chose to err on the side of additional length; in any case, the field lengths are easily adjusted. The "LengthofOcc" field is a calculated value based on the length of the value in the occur-rence field.

The interaction between script and the table passes through the Perl Database Interface (DBI) using the ODBC (Open Data-base Connectivity) database driver. This can easily be edited to use different drivers to connect to MySQL, Oracle, or other re-lational databases. The SQL statements have been deliberately kept generic, and we have chosen not to use stored procedures to improve portability.

The records are retrieved from the database, longest occur-rences first, and one by one the terms are matched against the document. Terms that have been tagged previously are ex-cluded: we don't want to match the "Halton" in "Halton Hills" if that term has already been tagged; nor do we want to match "Halton Hills" if "Halton Hills Public Library" has already been tagged. The <teiHeader> is ignored. Matching is case sensitive. Among the first documents we used for testing was one in which there were hundreds of ship names, all capitalized. It proved a simple—but not foolproof—way of distinguishing be-tween ships and their namesakes. Finally, we had the match pro-cess check for simple plurals (string + "s") and possessives (string + "'s"). Because of the way Microsoft and other parsers handled white space in the XSLT transformations, we also brought trailing punctuation inside the tag.

The result of this process is a block of text like the following, from *Early Days in Richmond Hill*:

```
<name reg="Miles, Abner" type="person">Miles,</name> for example, opened the
community's first hotel and bequeathed his name to the rise of land first called <name
reg="Miles' Hill" type="place">Miles' Hill.</name>. <name reg="Kinnear, Thomas"
type="person">Kinnear,</name> on the other hand, passed into history as the town's
most illustrious murder victim.
```

Without question, populating the names table is the most tedious part of the exercise, and for us it has been an amalgam of several approaches: cut and paste from the document, import unique values from other data structures that are well formed or naturally occurring, migrate indexes from other electronic documents. The regularization of names is an editorial decision, not a technical one, with one exception. It is essential that the terms being placed in the "reg" field comply with the encoding schema used for the document. For example a plain & (e.g., "Zimmerman, Samuel & Company") is perfectly legal in relational databases, but in the XML document the ampersand needs to be expressed as & (the same holds true for accented letters and a variety of other characters). The inverted form in which the Zimmerman company name is expressed represented a further editorial decision we made. Searching our indexes for "Samuel" will still find it, but we concluded that it had greater value in the browsable indexes if placed in the "Z" section.

At this point, one should have a valid TEI document with some number of <name> elements in it. Adding <index> and <rs> elements, for us, remains a manual process under the control of the indexer. It would be possible to search these terms in place, or more likely, to employ an XML indexing tool to aid in context-sensitive searching. In our case, part of the indexing strategy was to merge the indexes from our electronic collection into a preexisting meta-index of one of our collections. The fact that we might never have the rights to produce electronic versions of these publications does not reduce their value to the researcher. Indeed, given the narrowing of researcher interest in those items in the meta-index, one of our concerns was to ensure that the rest of the collection was adequately represented in the electronic tools. Consequently, our approach has been to extract index references into a relational database for purposes of searching. This has the added benefit, across a selection of documents (not all of which may return results for a given search term), of a positive impact on performance (or, to put it more bluntly, it reduced the potential additional burden on servers that are already overwhelmed with the volume of demand).

Index Extraction

From a valid TEI document, <name>, <index>, and <rs> elements are extracted and placed in a table. Subsequently, various CGI programs can be built to manage the search process and build URLs for retrieval of appropriate parts of the various documents.

The index table is defined as follows:

```
CREATE TABLE IndexTable (
    IndexID int,
    Subject1 char (100),
    Subject2 char (100),
    Type char (50),
    Context char (200),
    Illustration bit,
    SeeAlso char (50),
    PubCode char (50),
    DetailID char (8),
    SectionID char (8))
```

Subject1 receives the reg value from <rs> and <name>, and the level1 attribute from <index>.

Subject2 receives levels2 through 4 of <index>.

Type is type from <name type="x">.

Context is the extracted text value from the higher level <p>, <lg>, <note>, or <divx> with 50 characters before and after taken and trimmed off to the nearest space. The html <strong> element then surrounds the value.

Illustration sets a flag if the occurrence is within the <figure> element.

Search Results

Search: [   ] [Go!]   Your search for **Z** returned **103** entries.

Table of Contents

Zealand (8)
Zealand family (3)
Zealand, Captain (6)
Zealand, Edward Jr. (7)
Zealand, Edward L. (2)
Zealand, Edward Sr. (15)
Zealand, Henry (4)
Zealand, Miss (1)
Zealand, Mrs. (1)
Zealand, Thomas (1)
Zealand, W. (4)
Zealand, W. O. (2)
Zealand, William (9)
Zealand's Wharf (21)
Zebra (1)
Zephyr (1)
Zimmerman (11)
Zimmerman, Samuel (5)
Zimmerman, Samuel & Company (1)

Figure 6–1. *A screen shot of the index of Ivan S. Brookes's* History of Hamilton Harbour, *showing the Z section, the search box, the links to specific letters of the alphabet, and a Categories search (on the type attribute)*

DetailID is from the first "ID" encountered.

SectionID is from the <div2> or <div1> element.

SeeAlso is a column used to provide simple cross references within the index.

An index script populates the index table with these values, and then removes duplicates if there are multiple occurrences of Subject1, Subject2, or DetailID (in short, the same term tagged twice within a paragraph).

We should note that our data structure has grown more

complicated than this as we look at amalgamating this set of indexes with those derived from other data sources, such as transcribed newspaper articles.

PROBLEMS AND CHALLENGES, SUCCESSES AND FAILURES

Among the biggest challenges in building this project in 1999-2000 was the immaturity of the parsers in both Perl and the MSXML component common to most Microsoft programming languages. This situation, at least so far as these tools push XML, is largely resolved as of this writing.

There is a disconnect between the relational databases we used and the core XML entities. When you cut and paste from a document that displays & (the ampersand) the paste enters a plain & and not the required &. We routinely did a conversion in the database, but it ultimately proved more reliable to convert into the proper entity declaration on the fly.

The process of populating the name lookup table remains the most time-consuming process, especially at the start. It is possible to copy a wide variety of content from other databases. The result of a batch process can still lead to some interesting results. One ship database brought with it references to the *May*. Two schooners of this name graced the waters of Lake Erie prior to the Civil War. This example represents all that this project might hope to achieve: without name tagging, the vessels are blocked in most search engines' stopword lists or lost in an overwhelming set of irrelevant hits. On the other hand, automatically tagging each reference to the strings *May* and *MAY* brings its own challenges.

It remains to be seen how static the XML marked-up documents remain. In the library field, we know that thesaures are living things. In a relational database, our subject headings can be live pointers to the subject authority table, so that updates are instantly (or reasonably quickly) passed on to the associated record. The XML documents in the corpus have a life independent of any authority control linkages that we might establish, which is not to say that various batch processes cannot be established to maintain the copy that stays at home. In particular, the "key" attribute exists as a potential pointer to an external subject and name authority file.

Finally, the process remains semiautomated. Like those programs that aspire to translate between languages, the best we hope to accomplish is to expedite the work of a knowledgeable indexer. Someone who actually knows the subject material is still essential to the task of interpreting cryptic but potentially relevant references. Unlike most indexers in the traditional publishing trades, those who deal with public domain texts are not in a position to discuss ambiguous constructions with the authors because they have been dead the requisite number of years. That said, these tools make it possible to disambiguate thousands of reference points across multiple texts in a fraction of the time that doing this process with "traditional" XML editing tools would have required. And the net result is to improve relevance dramatically.

PLANS

The next steps for this particular set of projects consist largely of adding to the corpus of documents.

IMPLICATIONS

When would this approach be of most value? It is of particular relevance in dealing with a collection of nonfiction material with a focus. We applied it to a series of local histories and to a collection of texts on the maritime history of the Great Lakes. In both instances the ability to leverage the name lookup table from one document to the next means that the savings increase as the project moves forward. The biggest cost is in the first volume. Within that context, the greatest value is derived from work on name-intensive narratives. It proved significantly more challenging to tag concepts than proper names.

Finally, for our work, it was also important to find ways to integrate indexes from volumes that the rights to digitize have been refused or when the copyright owners are nowhere to be found. This also has the advantage of supporting documents that were imaged rather than transcribed, although little of what we have said about automated markup is relevant in the latter case.

CONTACTS

Walter Lewis
lewisw@hhpl.on.ca

Gail Richardson
gailrichardson@sympatico.ca

Geoffrey Cannon
cannong@hhpl.on.ca
Halton Hills Public Library
9 Church St.
Georgetown, ON
L7G 2A3
(905) 873-2601

LINKS AND RESOURCES

Early Days in Richmond Hill
edrh.rhpl.richmondhill.on.ca/
This site serves a substantial recent local history marked up using the tools this article describes. The original volume was 400 printed pages.

Maritime History of the Great Lakes
www.hhpl.on.ca/GreatLakes/
This site includes several documents using this technology. At writing there were more than 18,000 index references among the documents.

Text Encoding Initiative Consortium
www.tei-c.org
The best place to start an exploration of TEI is at the source.

The scripts are available on the HALINET Web server:
www.library.hhpl.on.ca/XML/

Application IV

USING XML TO
BUILD COLLECTIONS

IN LIBRARIES

When some librarians think of XML, they naturally think of the two purposes to which its predecessor, SGML, was put. SGML has been used in libraries to encode only two kinds of information: (1) archival finding aids and (2) full-text documents, such as books. As we have seen in this book, however, XML is being used for many other purposes for which SGML was too cumbersome a tool.

In Chapter 7, "Using XML to Federate Collections," Heidi Schmidt demonstrates the flexibility of XML in dealing with a massive collection of documents for which no unified set of descriptors exists.

Some of the same strengths that make XML a more all-purpose tool than SGML also make it well suited for some of the same tasks for which SGML had previously been the solution of choice. The second chapter in this section, "Publishing Books Online at eScholarship," describes a classic case of putting books online using structured markup. However, similarities to previous projects using SGML end there. Roy Tennant demonstrates some capabilities of XML that were not previously possible using an SGML infrastructure—such as dynamic displays controlled by the user. It's clear from these projects that building online collections isn't what it used to be. Nor will it likely ever be again.

7

Using XML to Federate Collections: The Legacy Tobacco Documents Library

Heidi Schmidt
University of California, San Francisco

BACKGROUND

The Master Settlement Agreement between the National Association of Attorneys General (NAAG) and six major tobacco companies resulted in millions of tobacco industry documents becoming available to the public. Under terms of the settlement, the tobacco companies are required to deposit paper copies of their documents in the Minnesota State Archive until 2008, and to make electronic copies available via the Web until 2010. In 2001, the American Legacy Foundation awarded the University of California San Francisco Library/Center for Knowledge Management (the Library) a grant to create a permanent electronic archive for the documents and a unified search interface for the entire collection of more than 20 million pages. The basis of the Legacy Tobacco Documents Library (LTDL) was a set of tapes created by the tobacco companies in the summer of 1999 and given to the Library through NAAG and the American Legacy Foundation.

PROJECT GOALS AND JUSTIFICATION

Although terms of the Master Settlement Agreement created the paper depository in Minnesota and require tobacco companies to make documents available online, each company maintains its own documents Web site. The multiplicity of sites, the differences between them, and occasional changes in site behavior make it difficult to build a single search interface for all the industry documents. In addition, companies can remove from their sites those documents related to pending litigation. The purpose of the Legacy Tobacco Documents Library is to have a single, permanent, online archive of tobacco documents released through the Master Settlement Agreement and to make the documents readily available to the public for research and education.

PROJECT DESCRIPTION

With two exceptions, the Legacy Tobacco Documents Library uses open-source software. The exceptions are XPAT, the search engine, which is licensed through the Digital Library Extension Service (DLXS) at the University of Michigan, and the Solaris operating system.

Operating System:	Solaris
Database:	PostgreSQL
Scripting Language:	Perl
Search Engine:	XPAT
Digital Library Tool Kit:	DLXS
Web Server:	Apache
Statistics Package:	Analog

The project team did not engage in a lengthy process to evaluate digital library toolkits. With a relatively large collection of documents, the team was particularly concerned with the performance and capabilities of the search engine and the feasibility of a small technical staff delivering all the desired features in one year. The DLXS/XPAT architecture developed by the University of Michigan was chosen because of its proven performance in large digital library projects and because it is

Field Name	Format	Max Length	Length Vary?	Nullable?	Unique?
document id	^.+$	24	true	false	true
document range	^.+$	29	true	true	false
author	^.+$	3924	true	true	false
recipient	^.+$	3898	true	true	false
copied	^.+$	1753	true	true	false
names mentioned	^.+$	63621	true	true	false
document date	^.+$	9	true	true	false
estimated date	^.+$	8	true	true	false
document type	^.+$	94	true	true	false
condition	^.+$	77	true	true	false
title	^.+$	1756	true	true	false
request number	^.+$	162	true	true	false
prod box	^.+$	7	true	true	false
date produced	^.+$	28	true	true	false
other bates numbers	^.+$	212	true	true	false
pages	^.+$	4	true	true	false
source	^.+$	161	true	true	false
description	^.+$	1322	true	true	false
case name	^.+$	49	true	false	false
ending date	^.+$	10	true	true	false
litigation usage	^.+$	133	true	true	false
date loaded	^[0-9]+$	8	false	false	false

Figure 7–1. *Schema file for Tobacco Institute documents*

based on components—Solaris, Perl, Apache, PostgreSQL—with which Library technical staff already had considerable expertise. DLXS staff took a sample set of tobacco industry documents and demonstrated how quickly DLXS tools could build search interfaces with both collection-specific and cross-collection searching, field-level search terms, and Boolean operators. The project team was impressed by the performance of XPAT and its integration with DLXS.

In January 2001, the Library received a set of 40 tapes containing image and document index files from seven tobacco companies. Data management consumed considerable effort during the initial phase of the project. Files were read from tapes and transferred to the target system. Image files had to be renamed for case consistency and loaded into file systems according to specific requirements of the DLXS software.

Programmers extracted field definition information from the document indexes of each document set and created schema files. Figure 7–1 shows the schema for Tobacco Institute documents. Perl scripts used schema files to load document records into PostgreSQL tables.

After the records were loaded, Perl scripts generated XML from the database. The XML design guidelines were:

- Implement uniform tag names for all document collections to simplify the architecture and avoid DLXS constraints.
- Use very short tag names—the XML files are enormous.
- Loosely correlate the tag name to its meaning—for example, "r" for recipients, "m" for names mentioned.
- Where necessary, use tag names expected by DLXS—for example, "YR" for date, "L" for author.

The XML generation process used customized map files. Here is an example of XML map code ("merge" and "map" are local Perl scripts):

```
. . . .
Merge doc_begin into bates_number.
Merge doc_end into bates_number.
Merge alias_begin into alias_bates.
Merge alias_end into alias_bates.
Map pnoted to n t="p".
Map onm to br t="o".
Map obrand to nothing.
Map bates_number to br t="p".
Map docdt to YR.
Map production_date to dp.
Map pauthor to L t="p".
Map grant_numbers to gn.
. . . .
```

The merge function accommodates differences in data format between collections. Most companies use a single field for the Bates number range of a document, while some companies

Display Name	XML tag	Philip Morris elements	Tobacco Institute elements	Lorillard elements
Title	K.	Verbatim Title	Title	Title
Author (Personal and corporate)	L.	Person Author, Org Author	Author	Person Author, Org Author
Recipient (Personal and corporate)	r.	Person Recipient, Org Recipient	Recipient	Person Recipent, Org Recipient
Copied (Personal and corporate)	c.	Person Copied, Org Copied	Copied	Person Copied, Org Copied
Mentioned Names (Personal and corporate)	m.	Person Mentioned, Org Mentioned	Names Mentioned	Person Mentioned, Org Mentioned
Document Date	dd.	Document Date	Document Date	Document Date
Document Type	dt.	Primary Type, Other Type	Document Type	Primary Type, Other Type
Condition	co.	Characteristics	Condition	Characteristics
Case Name	cn.		Case Name	
Litigation Useage	lu.	Litigation Useage	Litigation Useage	Litigation Useage
Request Number	rn. (and orn.?)	Request Number	Request Number	Request Number
Brand*	b.	Old Brand, Primary Brand, Mentioned Brand		Old Brand, Primary Brand, Mentioned Brand
Person Noted	n.	Person Noted, Org Noted		Person Noted, Org Noted
Attending	at.	Person Attending, Org Attending		Person Attending, Org Attending

Figure 7–2. Field mapping example

use separate fields for beginning Bates number and ending Bates number. (Bates numbers identify documents in legal cases.)

In the LTDL XML, there is only one tag attribute, "type." The type attribute is used to accommodate differences in data granularity between record formats of different tobacco companies. Some companies have only one field for "names mentioned," while others have separate fields for "persons mentioned" or "companies mentioned." The inclusive LTDL tag for "names mentioned" is <m>, but the attribute t can be set to "p," for example, to note this is a "person mentioned."

The next phase of the project was one of the most intellectually challenging. From the beginning, the Library was committed to two almost contradictory goals: to preserve the original material as received from the tobacco companies, and to provide searching across all document sets. Achieving both goals was difficult because document records received by the tobacco companies were inconsistent in format, range of fields, field names, and formats for dates and other information. The sample spreadsheet in Figure 7–2 demonstrates how the project team mapped fields from different document sets onto a set of common search options.

While normalizing search terms was required to create a common search interface for seven different document sets, the Library also wanted to provide advanced researchers the ability to search fields in individual document sets as they appeared in the source material, and as they are indexed on industry Web sites. Fortunately, DLXS provides this capability. After XML-tagged files are generated, XPAT indexes are created. In the DLXS environment, a configuration file maps search terms selected by the user to XPAT search strings. Here is part of a DLXS map file:

```
. . .
<mapping>
<label>mentioned names</label>
<synthetic>mentioned names</synthetic>
<native>region m</native>
<nativeregionname>m</nativeregionname>
<summarylabel>mentioned</summarylabel>
</mapping>
<mapping>
<label>mentioned persons</label>
<synthetic>mentioned persons</synthetic>
<native>(region m incl "t=p")</native>
<nativeregionname>m</nativeregionname>
<summarylabel>mentioned</summarylabel>
</mapping>
<mapping>
<label>mentioned organizations</label>
<synthetic>mentioned organizations</synthetic>
<native>(region m incl "t=o")</native>
<nativeregionname>m</nativeregionname>
<summarylabel>mentioned</summarylabel>
</mapping>
. . .
```

Figure 7–3 illustrates the normalized, cross-collection set of searchable fields. The different set of searchable fields available for a specific tobacco company—Brown and Williamson—is shown in Figure 7–4.

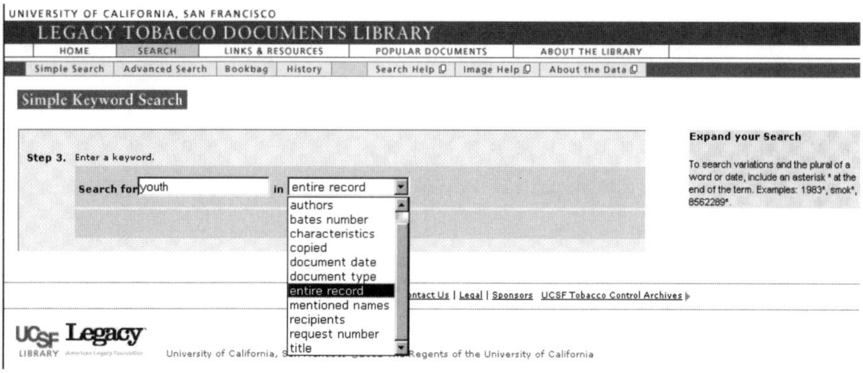

Figure 7–3. *Normalized search fields*

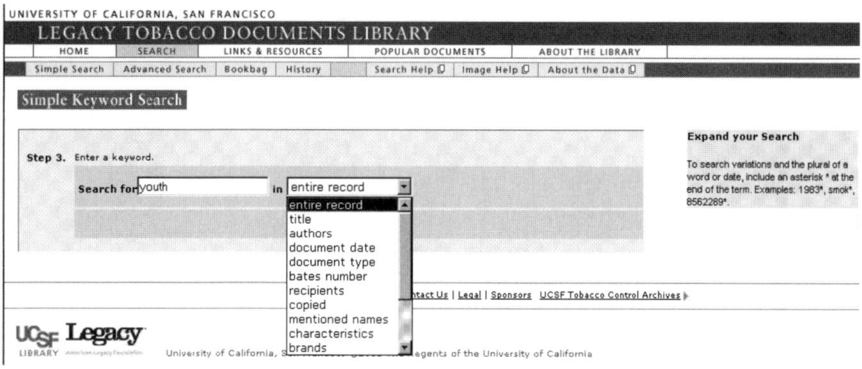

Figure 7–4. *Brown and Williamson–specific search terms*

PROBLEMS AND CHALLENGES, SUCCESSES AND FAILURES

The UCSF Library/Center for Knowledge Management met its objective of making approximately four million tobacco industry documents from the NAAG tapes available to the public through a common search interface in one year. The homepage and cross-collection search page are shown in Figures 7–5 and 7–6.

This achievement was particularly remarkable because the project team did not have access to the source material until the one-year development cycle started. As a banker once said, "A small number times a big number is still a big number." With a large document collection, even simple operations take a long

Figure 7–5. *Legacy Tobacco Documents Library homepage*

time. In building the LTDL, such operations included transferring files from tape to disk, moving files to target directories,
changing file name cases, generating XML, and XPAT indexing.

The technical team was also challenged in implementing the
DLXS tools. The LTDL could not have been built in one year
without the generosity of the University of Michigan in sharing code and providing their expertise. UCSF programmers
were frustrated, though, by the lack of DLXS documentation
and the idiosyncratic behavior of some of its modules. The decision was made to move forward with DLXS because it avoided
the delays inherent in a major software development effort, it
was designed to work with the quite satisfactory XPAT search
engine, and its use of XML mapping provided needed flexibility. On the other hand, the LTDL DLXS environment was customized to the point where the project team is wary of implementing DLXS upgrades without extensive testing in a costly
development environment.

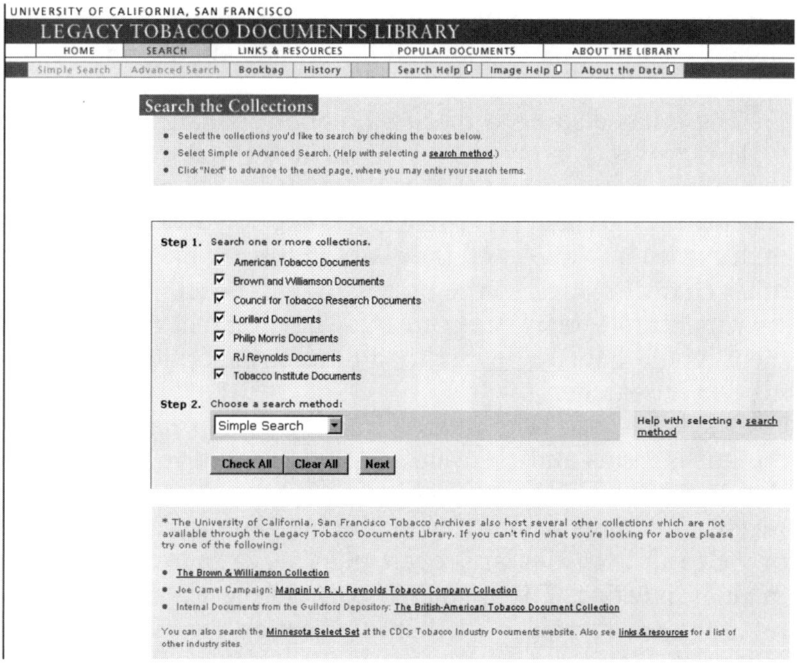

Figure 7–6. *Legacy Tobacco Documents Library main search page*

PLANS

Although the Legacy Tobacco Documents Library opened to the public on January 30, 2002, further effort is needed to ensure its integrity and completeness. The next phase of LTDL development will include exhaustively testing the correspondence between every document record and every document image received on the tapes. At launch, a small percentage of documents was missing, incomplete, or damaged. In the next phase of LTDL development, the project team will attempt to find the missing material on industry sites. There will also be an effort to collect documents released by the tobacco companies since the source tapes were made in July 1999.

A more complex future undertaking will involve integrating the LTDL, existing UCSF Tobacco Control Archives, and future collections of materials related to tobacco control. Without compromising the historical integrity of each document set, the

Library will explore options for cross-collection searching and streamlined user navigation while normalizing the underlying schemata and storage systems.

There has also been discussion about enhancing LTDL in various ways. One proposal is to process the documents with optical character recognition (OCR) software to create searchable text. The challenges are considerable, however. The volume of documents is large, and they vary in format, orientation, and other characteristics, so the process would be either very slow, very inaccurate, or very expensive. The digital library environment would have to be modified to offer the option of including text in searches.

There has also been interest in adding information such as thesaurus terms and abstracts to the document records. Given the size of the LTDL, manual indexing would be too costly. A review of automatic indexing methodologies indicates they rely on "clean" text files and even then serve only to augment manual indexing. The Library is considering ways to incorporate thesaurus terms and other information contributed by researchers using small document sets, but mechanisms are needed to distinguish this information from the original material. As these challenges are met, the abstraction provided by an XML-based information architecture will be essential in developing effective solutions.

TIPS AND ADVICE (LESSONS LEARNED)

The technical aspects of developing the Legacy Tobacco Documents Library required patience and technical expertise, but the intellectual components required discussion, documentation, and a decision-making hierarchy because consensus was not always possible. Discussions about normalizing date formats, for example, took more than a week! The project team was ultimately successful because it included a librarian, a technical architect, programmers, a system administrator, and a manager. The team met at least once a week, exchanged e-mail at a furious rate, and engaged in countless "over the cubicle wall" discussions.

IMPLICATIONS

This project proved the effectiveness of using a traditional database environment, XML, and XML-aware open-source digital library tools to preserve the integrity of source material while using different layers of normalization to maximize access to the collection for varying levels of user sophistication and research requirements. Not only is XML itself "extensible," but using XML was a key to creating an extensible architecture for the LTDL itself.

CONTACTS

Heidi Schmidt
Director, Academic Information Systems
Library/Center for Knowledge Management
University of California, San Francisco
530 Parnassus Avenue
San Francisco CA 94143-0840
(415) 514-0186

LINKS AND RESOURCES

Legacy Tobacco Document Library
www.legacy.library.ucsf.edu
The Legacy Tobacco Document Library is the product of the work described in this chapter.

PostgreSQL
www.postgresql.org
PostgreSQL is an open-source, object-relational DBMS that supports most SQL constructs.

Tobacco Control Archives
www.library.ucsf.edu/tobacco/
The UCSF Library/Center for Knowledge Management Tobacco Control Archives contain tobacco control document collections that preceded the LTDL. One of the Library's objectives is to

develop integrated search capabilities for all its materials related to tobacco control.

University of Michigan Digital Library Extension Service
www.dlxs.org
The University of Michigan Digital Library Extension Service makes the DLXS digital library tools available at no charge. DLXS also licenses the XPAT search engine to educational institutions.

American Legacy Foundation
www.americanlegacy.org
The American Legacy Foundation sponsored the work described in this chapter. Created by the 1998 Master Settlement Agreement, the Foundation is dedicated to reducing tobacco use.

8

Publishing Books Online at eScholarship

Roy Tennant
California Digital Library

BACKGROUND

The eScholarship initiative of the California Digital Library is teaming up with scholars to experiment with new modes of scholarly communication. Our strategy is to provide scholars with the infrastructure and services they need to try methods that we hope will prove to be faster and more effective than print-based communication. We also aim to provide long-term access to their scholarship through providing robust, fault-tolerant systems and data migration services.

One part of this effort is to publish books online. Beginning with a set of legacy titles, we sought to devise an infrastructure that offers innovative services for these titles while also providing the means by which we can easily migrate them into the future as technology changes. We settled on XML as a means to both ends.

PROJECT GOALS AND JUSTIFICATION

The goals of our project are to:

- maximize the present utility and long-term sustainability of the books, and

- provide innovative ways for users to interact with the texts (e.g., allow users to create their own alternative displays).

Publishing books online can be a complicated and time-consuming process. As technology changes, the books may need to be migrated from one format to another. The best strategy for preventing a complicated migration process is to store the book in an open, machine-parsable format like XML. Not only can we alter what the user sees without touching the book itself, but we can also process the book programmatically to change the text encoding if that is necessary in the future.

Also, we believe that online publishing provides new opportunities to respond to user needs. Some users have difficulty reading normal-size text on a screen, or indeed reading text by sight at all. Therefore, we also wanted to create an infrastructure that would allow the user to select how the item is viewed without creating multiple separate versions of the text. In our model, the text exists only once, in a canonical form encoded in XML, and different presentation formats can be applied to the text in batch mode or on the fly for different needs.

We also sought to provide powerful searching options that would allow a user to first discover which book mentioned a topic of interest, and then to "drill down" into the text to find the specific parts in which that topic was discussed.

PROJECT DESCRIPTION

The books are marked up in XML using a tag set that draws upon ISO 12083 and TEI Lite. Some of the books were translated with Perl scripts from SGML, while others were translated from publisher formats such as QuarkXpress. They are stored as a single XML file per book, with any associated illustrations (e.g., photographs) as separate files.

To serve the books to the Web, we use the Cocoon Publishing Framework. The components of this are:

1. a Web server (we use Apache)
2. a Java servlet engine (we use Tomcat)
3. Cocoon.

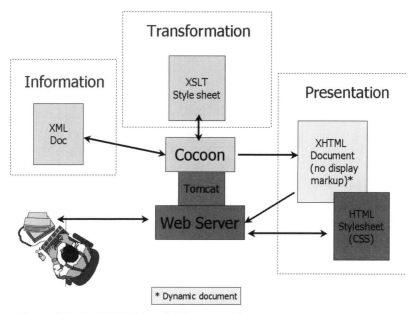

Figure 8–1. *An XML Web publishing model*

Tomcat is compiled into Apache, and provides a container within which Java servlets run. Cocoon is a Java servlet that allows you to call and run a specific Extensible Stylesheet Language Transformations (XSLT) style sheet against the document, which in turn can output straight HTML to the browser. This method of serving XML files means that users do not need any special browser or plug-in to view the book. Another software platform we are reviewing is AxKit, which performs the same function but in a mod_perl environment rather than Java.

This architecture allows online publishers to separate the content from how it is transformed and presented to the user (see Figure 8–1).

In this model, the content (or Information) can be rendered in any number of ways and yet remain untouched. Each XML-encoded book is associated with an XSLT style sheet that contains a series of rules and actions (the Transformation part of Figure 8–1). When the user requests the XML document, the associated style sheet is processed and the actions for any applicable rules are executed.

For example, if no chapter is specified when the book is requested, the user receives the table of contents and other prefatory material. If a particular chapter is requested, the style sheet will provide that chapter along with standard top and bottom button bars or text blocks that provide context as well as appropriate navigational choices (forward, back, etc.). The XSLT style sheet also translates the XML markup to XHTML on the fly, which can be viewed by standard Web browsers. Part of the XHTML that the XSLT style sheet outputs is a pointer to a default HTML Cascading Style Sheet (CSS) that defines exactly how the book should be displayed in a Web browser. Below I describe a method by which we also allow users to define display style sheets (CSS) to their specifications.

PROBLEMS AND CHALLENGES, SUCCESSES AND FAILURES

Searching

Searching was our primary challenge. Our goal is to provide robust but easy-to-use searching within a book as well as across all books, depending on the context and the need.

We began by trying the free utility "sgrep," which allows search words to be limited to various file segments such as section headings. The main limitation of using sgrep is that only one chapter can be searched at a time.

When the user searches the book, what is returned in response are any document segments (such as paragraphs) in which the search word(s) occur. The search words are highlighted. Clicking on a highlighted search word will jump to the location of that document segment within the full text of the chapter, which is displayed below the search results.

Our second attempt erased the limitation of searching only a chapter at a time, but it did not allow us to present document segments such as paragraphs to the user. Instead, a link to the chapter in which the search words occur is presented. This type of display is useful when searching across the entire collection, but is less useful when searching one book or when the user wants to find the exact location of the search words in the book.

To offer this type of searching, we switched from sgrep to SWISH-E, a free open-source application for indexing files of numerous types. To make it work the way we wanted it to, we needed to write a short Perl program to divide each book into chapter segments for the purpose of indexing (they are raw XML and are not displayed to the user). To facilitate the development and debugging process, we created Unix shell scripts to remove all the segmented files and re-create them again.

In our third attempt, we finally arrived at the solution we were hoping to reach from the outset. From the beginning, we believed the most desirable solution for searching would be to present a staged display to the user when searching across the entire collection. That is, initially the user would be presented with a list of all the books that match the search words. Clicking on a specific book would show the individual paragraphs of that book that matched the search, displayed within the context of the particular chapter in which it was found. Links would be available should the user wish to see the matched segments in the context of the entire chapter, or to browse the entire book.

We finally achieved this by using two different indexing programs and a Perl script, while presenting a single, unified interface to the user. We have set up two ways in which users can search the books:

1. If they click on the "Search" button while viewing a particular book, we assume they want to search the book they're viewing, in which case the search form automatically reflects that choice. They have the option, however, to broaden their search to all the books.
2. If they click on the "Search" button without viewing a particular book, we assume they wish to search across the collection.

To provide searching across the entire collection, we use SWISH-E. It is fast, and can quickly identify which book contains the search words. The search results are displayed as a set of matching titles, each with two choices: (1) view the search words in context or (2) browse the entire book (see Figure 8–2).

If the user selects the second choice (browse the book), he is simply forwarded to the location of that book for browsing.

Figure 8–2. Initial search results return matching books; from here, the user could select to view the search words in context (see Figure 8–3) or browse the entire book.

If the user selects the first choice (view search words in context), the search is forwarded to the second search application, XYZFind. This program returns only matching paragraphs, which are then displayed to the user within the context of the chapter and book from which they have been extracted (see Figure 8–3).

A Perl program provides the search form, passes the search to SWISH-E to locate matching books, presents these results to the user, passes the search on to XYZFind, and reformats the results.

Although we had a few false starts with solving our searching problem, we are pleased that we were able to achieve our vision of how searching should work—even if it takes using two indexing programs working together to pull it off.

Figure 8–3. *What the user sees after clicking on the "View search words(s) in context" choice.*

User-Defined Style Sheets

One of our goals is to allow those with sight issues to select the particular display that they find most effective. To do this, we needed a way that users could make style selections from a Web form, have the style sheet written out to a file, and then point all subsequent screen displays of that book to the user-created style sheet.

When the user initially requests a book, the default display for that title is shown (for example, see Figure 8–4). A link on the page will point to the form that allows the user to create a different style. Traveling that link executes a CGI program (written in Perl). Because the link was traveled from a particular book, the name of the book is passed as a parameter to the program. If the parameter is missing, the user is presented with a list of books for which alternate displays can be created. Once

Figure 8–4. The default display of one of the titles

a book is selected, the user can then make selections of how the book should be depicted from a Web form (see Figure 8–5).

The user makes the appropriate selections and clicks the button. The program writes out a personal style sheet to a temporary file (the files are automatically purged on a weekly basis), and forwards the user to the online book with an additional parameter: the filename of the newly created style sheet. The XSLT style sheet checks for the existence of this parameter, and if it is present, substitutes it for the default style sheet. From that point forward, the parameter continues to be passed, so that as the user moves from chapter to chapter, the style continues to be applied (see Figure 8–6).

The XSLT syntax used for this process is as follows. First the variable is set up at the beginning of the XSLT style sheet:

```
<xsl:variable name="userstyle">
    <xsl:value-of select="$style"/>
</xsl:variable>
```

Address: http://escholarship.cdlib.org/cgi-bin/pickstyle.pl?book=edwards.xml&part=0

California
THE UNIVERSITY OF CALIFORNIA PRESS E-EDITIONS

eScholarship

SEARCH

California
E-EDITIONS

Create Your Own Publication Style

Border Color:	White	
Background Color:	White	
Font Family:	Serif	A A **A**
Text Size:	normal	A**AA**
Text Color:	Black	A A A

Show me the book in my style

Figure 8–5. *The interface for selecting a different display style for any of our online books*

Then in the particular template in which it applies, the following XSLT will either output an XHTML tag (shown below in bold) that calls the user-defined style sheet or one that calls the default style sheet.

```
<xsl:choose>
    <xsl:when test="$display = 'user-defined'">
        <link rel="stylesheet" type="text/css" href="BASEURLOFUSER-
DEFINEDSTYLESHEET{$userstyle}" />
    </xsl:when>
    <xsl:otherwise>
        <link rel="stylesheet" type="text/css" href="URLOFDEFAULTSTYLE
SHEET" />
    </xsl:otherwise>
</xsl:choose>
```

Figure 8–6. *A possible user-selected display of one of the books (large print, sans-serif font)*

A link to the next chapter is created in the XSLT style sheet (notice the use of variables to define the next file, whether the display is user defined or not, and the name of the user-defined style sheet if one exists):

```
<a href="{$nextfile}&amp;display={$display}&amp;
style={$userstyle}">Forward</a>
```

This would show up in the browser as:

```
<a href="filename.xml?part=4&display=user-defined&
style=992621580.564453.css">Forward</a>
```

Once we determine the best settings for those with particular sight issues, we will offer links from the front page of each book that will select a preconfigured style sheet so they need not go through the process of building their own. This will also allow users to bookmark the different display and have the setting retained (style sheets created by a user are erased after a week).

PLANS

On-the-Fly Creation of Adobe Acrobat Versions

A logical next step on the path of user-defined displays is to allow the user who has defined how the book will be displayed to be able to output an Adobe Acrobat version of the entire work in this format. This would then allow users to retain their views of the item longer than the default one week that style sheets will remain on our servers. It will also provide an easy method for printing out a full copy of the book in the desired format.

Variable Character Encodings Based on Browser

Although non-Roman characters are encoded in the books using the international Unicode standard, not all Web browsers can properly display them. We would like to send different character encodings to users based on the particular Web browser they are using, thereby optimizing the display for the limitations of that browser. But because Web browsers are becoming much better at displaying non-Roman character sets (e.g., Netscape 6 does a decent job), this soon may not be required.

TIPS AND ADVICE (LESSONS LEARNED)

At least at the time that we implemented it, the software infrastructure had stability issues as well as desired functionality that was missing. We found that serving entire books to the user was not advisable from the server viewpoint, holding aside questions of usability from the user's perspective. We realized we were somewhat on the "bleeding edge," but it seemed like the best tool for the job, and in fact met our goals fairly well overall. But if we could have waited a year or two until the software situation was better, it would likely have been less difficult and more effective.

We also learned that providing logical and effective search systems for books encoded in XML can be an art as much as it is a science. XML search options are not yet as fully developed as one might desire; therefore, constructing a robust search service requires more flexibility and imagination.

IMPLICATIONS

This project has proven the utility and importance of the basic model for publishing XML documents: the document remains in a highly structured, easily translatable format (therefore enhancing preservation options), while display transformations are applied to the document at the moment the user requests it, based on the user's specifications. This model allows the document to be stored once in a standard, authoritative format while also allowing endless transformations based on varying user needs. One person may wish to have a large-print version for reading online; another may wish to print it. Others might want to have it read out loud to them using screen-reading software. Each user should be able to retrieve a version that has been optimized for those different needs without altering the document itself.

XML, its related standards like XSLT, and a publishing framework such as Cocoon or AxKit, now make this possible. This project demonstrates that it is also achievable, desirable, and effective.

CONTACT

Roy Tennant
Manager, eScholarship Web & Services Design
California Digital Library
415 20th Street, 4th Floor
Oakland, CA 94612
(510) 987-0476
roy.tennant@ucop.edu

LINKS AND RESOURCES

AxKit
axkit.org
A Perl application for serving XML content to the Web. AxKit can use an XSLT style sheet to transform an XML document to HTML for delivery to a standard Web client.

The California Digital Library
www.cdlib.org
The digital library initiative of the University of California, and the organization that hosts the eScholarship effort.

Cocoon
xml.apache.org/cocoon/
A Java application for serving XML content to the Web. Cocoon can use an XSLT style sheet to transform an XML document to HTML for delivery to a standard Web client.

eScholarship
escholarship.cdlib.org/
An initiative of the California Digital Library that fosters scholar-led innovations in scholarly publishing. Current activities include electronic preprints, electronic journals, online datasets, and electronic books.

eScholarship "pickstyle" CGI Script
escholarship.cdlib.org/cgi-bin/pickstyle.pl
The script that allows individual readers to create their own display of books published online by eScholarship.

sgrep
www.cs.helsinki.fi/u/jjaakkol/sgrep.html
"Structured grep," a free utility for searching structured documents.

SWISH-E
sunsite.berkeley.edu/SWISH-E/
A free application for indexing documents.

TEI Lite
www.hcu.ox.ac.uk/TEI/Lite/
The Text Encoding Initiative's "lite" version of its document
type definition (DTD) for structural markup of monographs.

Tomcat
jakarta.apache.org/tomcat/
A Java servlet engine that is compiled into the Web server to
provide an environment in which Java applications can run resi-
dent in memory (rather than being bootstrapped every time a
user requests its services).

UC Press Books at eScholarship
escholarship.cdlib.org/ucpressbooks.html
A list of University of California Press books published online
by eScholarship.

Unicode
www.unicode.org
The international effort to specify computer codes to properly
represent all human languages.

XYZFind
www.xyzfind.com
An XML-aware database package.

Application V

USING XML IN DATABASES

IN LIBRARIES

XML is, at its heart, a tree structure: elements are nested inside of other elements. For example, a paragraph is nested within a chapter that is nested within a book. In XML, you speak of such a hierarchy as consisting of "parents" (the container) and "children" (the contained). Such relationships are foreign to databases, which have strictly defined relationships that are distinctly unhierarchical.

However, as is perhaps clear by the projects described in this book, you can encode nearly anything in XML, and hierarchical relationships are by no means a requirement of much of the data being encoded. Therefore, XML-encoded data may be logically stored and accessed by database systems that are ignorant of parent-child relationships.

CHAPTER 9

In Chapter 9, "Building XML Databases with Zope and Castor," Art Rhyno discusses the relative merits of two open-source database systems for storing and serving XML data.

9

Building XML Databases with Zope and Castor

Art Rhyno
University of Windsor

BACKGROUND

Databases have become well-established solutions for managing digital collections. Although the underlying architecture can vary widely, database systems provide a robust infrastructure for querying and maintaining diverse digital content. XML has fostered an incredible amount of technologies for content creation and presentation, but the options for storing XML in a database and providing a management layer are somewhat more limited, particularly for organizations with small budgets.

Database solutions for XML have become an area of active research at the Leddy Library at the University of Windsor. The Library is a partner with the Windsor Public Library and others in the Windsor-Essex Digitization Resource Framework, a collaborative framework for digitizing cultural and heritage collections, architectural materials, and historical artifacts for resource sharing and preservation. The Library is also a participant in several open-source library system initiatives, including the Open Source Digital Library System (OSDLS). XML is a key ingredient for all of these projects, while the scale of the systems being created argues for a database solution.

For reasons that will be explained, we have adopted two

very different approaches for storing XML in a database. Each is representative of one side of the debate over the best methods for leveraging database technology for use with XML, and they help illustrate why one solution may be preferred over another based on the nature of the content in the collection.

PROJECT GOALS AND JUSTIFICATION

The goals we have defined are:

- Make effective use of database technology for storing and providing a search engine for XML content.
- Define solutions that are based on open-source components.
- Create Web-enabled systems that will require minimum effort to serve content to Web browsers.

Maintaining an XML collection as a set of individual XML files can quickly become unwieldy as the collection grows, particularly if multiple users will be updating the files at the same time. Utilizing a database allows for a greater level of control in dealing with multiple updates and supports searching functions directly rather than relying on an external indexing program. As well, several outstanding open-source database systems are available, such as MySQL, which have a solid track record for managing large amounts of data.

Databases are also becoming a common back end to busy Web sites. Defining a strategy for database use with XML lays important groundwork for future XML-based Web services.

PROJECT DESCRIPTION

The project consists of mechanisms defined for two very different types of content. In one, historical materials are being made available on the Web, including a very large finding aid marked up in EAD (Encoded Archival Description). This finding aid consists of more than 14,000 lines of XML. For the other type of content, MARC (Machine Readable Cataloging), the widespread format for bibliographic information, and RDF (Resource Description Framework), the World Wide Web Consortium's

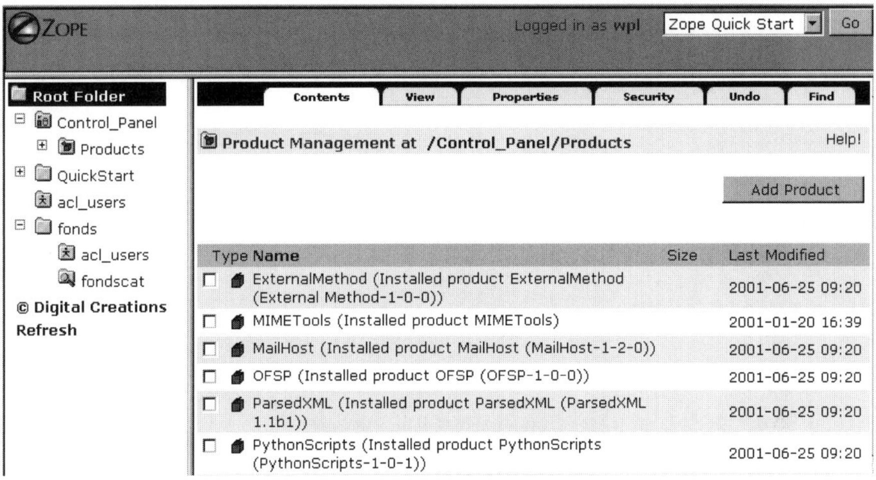

Figure 9–1. *The management interface in Zope lists currently installed products*

(W3C) standard for metadata, are brought together in an XML implementation. The EAD content is very text intensive, with many sections consisting of several paragraphs of text. The MARC/RDF metadata is much more concise, but will conceivably undergo more frequent updates and can consist of millions of individual records.

Zope for EAD

The EAD content is managed using Zope, the open-source Web application server from Digital Creations. Zope provides a built-in Web server and a Web-based management interface as well as scripting language support and an object database. In Zope parlance, components to be added to the server for additional functionality are called "products," and several XML-related products exist for Zope. The latest, called ParsedXML, utilizes the DOM (Document Object Module) for interacting with XML documents. DOM is an effort under the auspices of the W3C to standardize how programs can interact with Web documents. By using the DOM, an application can rely on a well-understood and documented technology for working with Web content.

One of the key advantages of a Zope application is that it

```
File  Edit  View  Go  Communicator  Help

ZOPE                                    Logged in as wpl   Zope Quick Start

Root Folder                  Script (Python) at /fonds/fondscat/walkTree
  Control_Panel
    Products           Title            Walk and Catalog DOM Tree
  QuickStart           Parameter List   nextChild,URLstr,URLstem
  acl_users            Bound Names      context, container, script, traverse_subpath
  fonds                Last Modified    2001-06-25 09:28
    acl_users          trackURL = URLstr
    fondscat           if nextChild.parentNode:
  Digital Creations        trackURL = trackURL + '/' + nextChild.tpURL()
  Refresh              else:
                           trackURL = nextChild.absolute_url() + trackURL

                       if nextChild.nodeValue:
                           if nextChild.nodeName == '#text':
                               #avoid blank nodes
                               if len(nextChild.nodeValue) > 1:
                                   container.catalog_object(nextChild,URLstem + trackURL)

                       if nextChild.hasChildNodes():
                           for child in nextChild.childNodes:
                               nextChild = container.walkTree(child,trackURL,URLstem)
```

Figure 9–2. *Simple Python script to catalog XML documents*

can tap into Zope's object database to provide searching capabilities. Zope exposes this capability through a product called Zcatalog, which is installed using Zope's Product Management interface (see Figure 9–1).

Zcatalogs maintain a collection of indexes; an index can be either full-text or based on predefined fields. A Zcatalog can be used to index many types of content in Zope with very little intervention beyond adding it through the product interface, but for our XML documents, we will choose to create a script to pass values directly to a full-text index. This allows very precise control over the indexing process, and we can take full advantage of the DOM structure. Zope supports Python and Perl scripting; the script we use (see Figure 9–2) is written in Python. The script is recursive and loops through each segment or "node" of an XML document.

Every node in ParsedXML has a unique URL, and the script determines what these are before passing the values to Zcatalog. The full-text index will allow the collection to be searched with Boolean expressions and simple wildcards, for example: report* AND speech*. When the search interface presents the results to

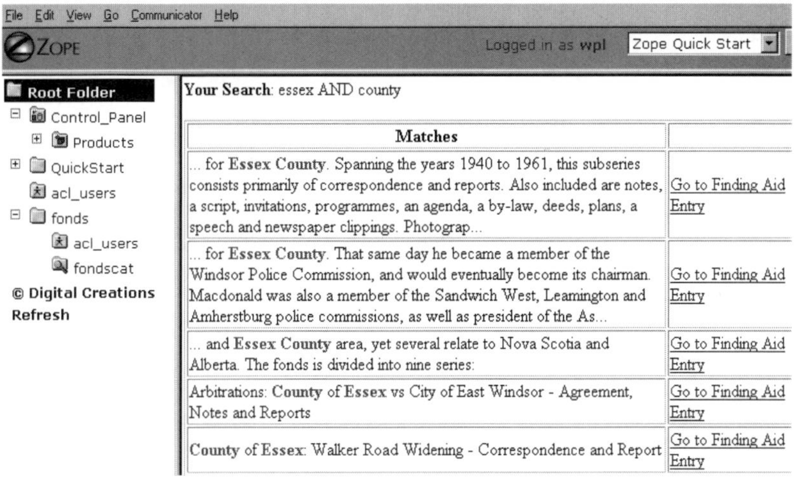

Figure 9–3. *A portion of each segment where search terms are found is displayed.*

a user, we are then able to display the node rather than the complete and often large XML document (see Figure 9–3).

Zope has numerous tools to manipulate content for Web services, and we are only beginning to delve into Zope's power to bring together a wider variety of formats in a browser environment. For example, integrating the XML content created for the finding aids with HTML documents authored for other collections within the Digital Alliance Framework would be possible within the search interface.

Castor for MARC and RDF

Castor is a Java-based XML Object/Relational Database (RDBMS) mapping tool. Unlike Zope, which stores an entire XML document in the database with all the tags and ordering preserved, Castor distributes pieces of an XML document to separate tables and assembles the XML representation "on the fly." The advantages and disadvantages of object databases as opposed to an RDBMS for storing XML are hotly debated, but the choice often comes down to the nature of the application. From a purely pragmatic perspective, an RDBMS tends to work

```
<!DOCTYPE databases PUBLIC "
-//EXOLAB/Castor Mapping DTD Version
1.0//EN"
"http://castor.exolab.org/mapping.dtd">
    <!— Mapping for Resource —>
    <class name="pytheas.Resource"
        identity="id">
        <description>Resource - network or
otherwise</description>
        <map-to table="resource" xml="resource" />
        <field name="id" type="integer" >
            <sql name="id" type="integer"/>
            <xml node="attribute"/>
        </field>
        <field name="uri" type="string">
            <sql name="uri" type="char"
                dirty="check" />
            <xml node="text" />
        </field>
    </class>
    <!— Mapping for Marc —>
    <class name="pytheas.Marc"
        identity="id">
        <description>Marc Variable tags</description>
        <map-to table="marc" xml="marc" />
        <field name="id" type="integer">
            <sql name="id" type="integer" />
        </field>
    <!— Additional mapping goes here —>
```

```
create table resource
( id int not null primary key,
uri varchar(255) not null);
grant all on resource to sa;

create table marc (
    id int not null primary key,
    resource_id   int not null,
    marc_type varchar(1)   not null,
    foreign key (resource_id)
        references resource( id ));

create unique index marc_pk on
    marc(id,resource_id);
grant all on marc to sa;

create table marc_tag (
    id int not null primary key,
    marc_id   int not null,
    tag varchar(3)  not null,
    ind1 varchar(1) not null,
    ind2 varchar(2) not null
    foreign key (marc_id)
        references marc( id ));

create unique index marc_tag_pk on
    marc_tag(id,marc_id);
grant all on marc_tag to sa;
```

Figure 9–4. *Castor uses the mapping file on the left to work with the tables defined on the right.*

well for very structured data that can be broken down into segments that do not typically exceed 255 characters. Although commercial databases like Oracle can expand this threshold for textual information, most open-source relational databases require textual fields greater than 255 characters to be either:

   1. stored as a BLOB (Binary Large Object), which greatly reduces the ability of an application to work with the data, or

2. broken into multiple fields, which requires that the application reassemble the field for many types of updates and interactions with client programs.

By working with the structure of RDF and MARC, we are able to define an XML view of our data that can usually abide by the 255-character limitation (see Figure 9–4).

Records going in and out of an RDBMS with Castor are structured according to this XML view. For example, given the title *Extreme games and their solutions* and an RDF statement concerning this work, the results can be presented and manipulated as an XML document:

```
<bib id="6">
        <marcType>B</marcType>
        <recordStatus>n</recordStatus>
        <recordType>a</recordType>
        <endcodingLevel>0</endcodingLevel>
        <!— Other fixed fields omitted —>
        <tag ind1="1" ind2="0">245
            <subf id="6" seq-no="0" subfCode="a">
Extreme Games and their solutions</subf>
            <subf id="7" seq-no="0" subfCode="c">
Joachim Rosenm&uuml;ller</subf>
        </tag>
        <!— Other variable fields omitted —>
        <subjectHeading id="9">
            <normalHeading>GAME THEORY</normalHeading>
        <!— Other headings omitted —>
        <resource id="3">
            <uri>http://localhost/servlets/pytheasXML?id=1</uri>
        </resource>
        <rdf>
            <nameSpace>
http://somewhere.org/recommendations</nameSpace>
            <predicate>recommendedBy</predicate>
            <value>John Smith</value>
        </rdf>
        <!— Other RDF statements omitted —>
</bib>
```

Castor is an example of a *data binding framework*, a way to map a data format to a specific and meaningful representation in a programming language, in this case XML to Java. Because it is Java-centric, Castor can be combined with other Java technologies, such as Web servlets, and can be plugged into an Enterprise Java Bean environment, which is a Java-based middleware infrastructure for building large applications. The net result of using Castor is that database records can be created and queried with a high level of abstraction in Java:

```
// Java fragment

Mapping  mapping;
JDO      jdo;

Database db;
Bib      bib;
MarcTag  tag;
MarcTagSubfsubf;
Rdf      rdf;
SubjHeading subjHeading;

// We will display everything on the standard output
PrintWriter writer = new Logger( System.out ).setPrefix( "pytheas" );

// Get mapping information from mapping.xml file
mapping = new Mapping( getClass().getClassLoader() );
mapping.setLogWriter( writer );
mapping.loadMapping( getClass().getResource("mapping.xml" ) );

// Configure and open the JDO database
jdo = new JDO();
jdo.setLogWriter( writer );
jdo.setConfiguration( getClass().getResource( "database.xml" ).toString() );
jdo.setDatabaseName( "test" );
db = jdo.getDatabase();
db.begin();

// Create a new Subject Heading
subjHeading = new SubjHeading();
```

```
subjHeading.addNormalHeading( "GAME THEORY" );
db.create( subjHeading );

// Create new Bibliographic Record
bib = new Bib();
bib.setMarctype( "b" );
bib.setRecordtype("a" );

// Create variable Marc tag entry
tag = new MarcTag();
tag.setInd1( "1" );
tag.setInd2( "0" );
tag.setTag ("245" );

// Add subfield
subf = new MarcTagSubf();
subf.setSeqNo( 0 );
subf.setSubfCode( "a" );
subf.setSubfValue( "Extreme Games and their solutions" );

// Add subfield to tag
tag.addSubf( subf );

// Add tag to Bib
bib.addTag( tag );

// Add Subject Heading to Bib
bib.addSubjHeading( subfHeading );

// Add Bib to the database
db.create( bib );

// Commit the transaction
db.commit();

// View and query our record using XML Mapping
Marshaller    marshaller;
OQLQuery    bibOql;
QueryResults    results;

marshaller = new Marshaller( writer );
marshaller.setMapping( mapping );
```

```
// There are numerous ways to query database, this example will use LIKE clause
bibOql = db.getOQLQuery( "SELECT b FROM pytheas.Bib b " +
"WHERE tags.subfs.subfValue LIKE \"%games%\"" );

// Based on the above query, we will now view all records returned
results = subfOql.execute();
while( results.hasMore() )
marshaller.marshal( results.next() );
```

Castor focuses on the way the database will store the data, and much of the business logic associated with an application may be found in an external DTD/schema rather than in the database's XML view. As long as the XML produced by an application meets the baseline XML defined for Castor, more rigorous validation can occur within an XML authoring tool that supports DTDs or using a schema. There are also tools like Schematron that allow for specifying additional constraints that do not fit neatly into a DTD/schema.

As can be seen in the above code fragment, Castor supports a query language called OQL (Object Query Language), which can be used instead of the traditional and much more cryptic Standard Query Language (SQL). For example, the query in the Java fragment in OQL is given as:

```
SELECT b FROM pytheas.Bib b WHERE tags.subfs.subfValue LIKE "%games%"
```

Compare this to using SQL directly, where the query becomes:

```
SELECT a2.id,marc.tag, marc.ind1, marc.ind2, marc.resource_id, marc_tag.id,
marc_subjheading_marc.heading_id, a2.marctype FROM bib a1 LEFT OUTER JOIN
marc_tag ON (a1.id=marc_tag.marc_id), bib a2 LEFT OUTER JOIN marc_heading_marc
ON (a2.id=marc_subjheading_marc.marc_id), marc_tag_subf, marc WHERE
a2.id=marc.id AND marc.id=marc_tag.marc_id AND marc_tag.id=marc_tag_subf.
marctag_id AND a2.id=a1.id AND marc_tag_subf.subf_value LIKE '%games%'
```

It is possible to pass SQL directly to the underlying database if desired, but a key advantage of Castor is that it can greatly simplify querying an RDBMS in addition to streamlining the process of updating records.

PROBLEMS AND CHALLENGES, SUCCESSES AND FAILURES

Life on the Cutting Edge

Like many open-source projects, Zope and Castor are frequently being updated. Zope itself is very stable at this point, but ParsedXML is quite new at the time of this writing and is still short on documentation. Castor is a much smaller project than Zope, although both initiatives share very dedicated developers and active mailing lists. Using ParsedXML and Castor requires experimentation and a willingness to work without glossy manuals and a vendor support center. In order to handle the complexity of MARC in OQL queries, for example, it was necessary to modify the Castor parser to correct some odd behavior involving table names. Fortunately, the Castor Web site and mailing list have evolved into excellent information sources, and the Zope community is legendary for its ability to share information on Zope applications.

Implementation Issues

Indexing a very large ParsedXML document in the Zope database can be quite time-consuming, but this kind of process can run in the background on most machines. Castor is database independent, but it requires transaction and outer join support in the RDBMS. Open-source options for using Castor include PostgreSQL 7.1 (or higher), MySQL 3.23 (or higher), and HypersonicSQL.

We have not used the functionality of ParsedXML to support a more refined editing environment. Documents for our project tend to be authored in other environments and do not see much updating after they are received. For many XML projects, it is quite likely that Zope's strong features for maintaining content across disparate locations would be well worth investigating. The relationships between MARC and XML, as well as XML and RDF schema, are still being defined at this point; it is expected that refinements will need to be made to our Castor mappings as the library community explores the use of XML in library services.

PLANS

We want to use XSLT for displaying HTML to Web browsers across all projects. In Zope, support for this is being added to ParsedXML through a product called XSLTemplate, although there are options for integrating Zope with Apache that would allow the use of Apache XML tools. Castor works well with Apache's tools, and we hope to combine our application with some third-party EJB programs into the open-source JBoss EJB server. We hope this will serve as a "proof of concept" that large systems can benefit from the middleware infrastructure provided by EJB and similar architectures.

TIPS AND ADVICE (LESSONS LEARNED)

The mailing lists for Zope/ParsedXML and Castor are archived and are well worth consulting. Most open-source projects have a CVS version (Concurrent Versions System) that can be either downloaded or browsed online, and it is often invaluable to read the comments about an application in the code itself.

It is also well worth identifying a machine that you can experiment on without causing your colleagues or the library's patrons any distress. Both Zope and Castor can be installed on Linux and most versions of Windows so that you can usually define and refine your application on whatever hardware is available without having to share processing resources with the library's other systems.

IMPLICATIONS

This project shows that storing XML in a database is viable without requiring a huge expenditure on the part of the library. By combining a database with XML tools, libraries can leverage mainstream technologies to create applications and use database technology to manage large XML collections.

CONTACT

Art Rhyno
Systems Librarian
Leddy Library, University of Windsor
401 Sunset Avenue
Windsor, ON N9B 3P4
(519) 253-3000, ext. 3163
arhyno@uwindsor.ca

LINKS AND RESOURCES

Castor
castor.exolab.org
An open-source XML data binding framework for Java.

Encoded Archival Description (EAD)
www.loc.gov/ead/
EAD is a nonproprietary encoding standard for finding aids such as inventories, registers, indexes, and other documents created by archives, libraries, museums, and manuscript repositories.

Enterprise JavaBeans Page
java.sun.com/products/ejb/
Sun's solution for the future of middleware and the premier technology for wiring together large systems in Java.

HypersonicSQL
sourceforge.net/projects/hsqldb/
An incredibly compact Java-based RDBMS that is small enough to be delivered in an applet.

Jboss EJB Project
www.jboss.org
JBoss is an open-source EJB project that features documented Castor integration. Commercial EJB servers are very expensive, making JBoss a much needed option for delving into EJB.

MySQL
www.mysql.com
One of the most popular databases in the world, MySQL is the backbone for many Web sites and is a favored option among open-source developers.

Open Source Digital Library System
osdls.library.arizona.edu/
The OSDLS is an effort to create an open-source Integrated Library System (ILS) and other library tools.

ParsedXML
www.zope.org/Members/faassen/ParsedXML
An advanced XML storage tool for Zope based on the Document Object Model.

PostgreSQL
www.postgresql.org/
Billed as the "world's most advanced Open Source Database," PostgeSQL is a full-featured and highly advanced database system.

Resource Description Framework (RDF)
www.w3.org/RDF/
RDF is a framework for metadata. It allows metadata to be packaged in XML based on a common vocabulary. Various research communities or groups with a common interest may define this common vocabulary in a schema.

Schematron
www.ascc.net/xml/resource/schematron/
This flexible tool for validating XML content is ideal for validation issues that do not fit neatly or are too complex to be handled in a traditional DTD or schema.

Windsor-Essex Digitization Resource Framework
www.windsorpubliclibrary.com/digi/
A collaborative project for building and supporting local history collections.

Zope

www.zope.org
One of the first and most popular Web application servers.

Application VI

USING XML FOR DATA MIGRATION

IN LIBRARIES

Given the fact that XML is still new on the scene, it should come as no surprise that data migration (moving information from one format to another) is an important issue. Our first chapter in this section illustrates a classic case of increasing the usability of information by migrating it from a less formal and strict standard (HTML) to one that is much more strict and therefore machine-parsable (XML).

CHAPTER 10

The purposes of the project described by Darlene Fitcher in Chapter 10, "Migrating Native Law Cases from HTML to XML" were to ensure long-term preservation of the cases, enhance their utility, and experiment with search and retrieval systems. Because it is likely that many libraries will find it necessary to migrate information encoded in HTML into the richer and more standardized XML encoding, the lessons from this project may be particularly instructive.

CHAPTER 11

However, lest you think that once you move your data from legacy systems into XML your troubles are over, our second chapter in this section, "Transforming Word Processing Documents into XML," is here to remind you differently. Despite the existence of XML, most people will continue to use off-the-shelf software such as Microsoft Word to create their documents. And the result of using such software (particularly in the way in which most users use it), is a file that is far from the kind of highly structured file that you may desire (and that can be easily encoded in XML). Therefore, Brian Rosenblum's contribution to this book is likely to be useful for quite some time, as the need to migrate information from word processing programs to XML is not likely to go away any time soon.

10

Migrating Native Law Cases from HTML to XML

Darlene Fichter
University of Saskatchewan Library

BACKGROUND

In 1994, the University of Saskatchewan Library started a project to enhance the access and delivery of library materials for native studies. We faced a three-fold challenge: increased demand for material, preservation issues, and barriers to access. On- and off-campus students were using reference and circulation materials more than ever before, and the print collection could not keep up with the heavy demand. Many items were wearing out and could not be replaced, others were lost or stolen. Some of the excellent primary and secondary materials in special collections were not easily accessed: locating single items contained in a collection of documents or photographs proved difficult. Search and retrieval by interested scholars and students was a time-consuming task.

We created the Resources for Aboriginal Studies site to ensure better access to native studies materials (http://library.usask.ca/native/). Figure 10–1 shows the project homepage. The University Archives and Library added item-level records for manuscript and photographs to a database to facilitate access. Full-text materials such as native law cases, documents, diaries, and broadsheets were digitized and mounted on a Web site. Photographs were scanned and added to a photographic database.

In 1993, the University of Saskatchewan Library was asked to make the electronic version of a nine-volume set of native law cases available online. The cases were provided in ASCII text format. The collection contained about 527 cases pertaining to Canadian native law from the 1800s to the 1970s. This collection was of primary interest to the disciplines of native studies, history, and law. In 1994 and 1995, the law cases were converted to HTML and posted to the Web to enhance access and use. At that time SGML was considered as a possible repository format; due to budget constraints and the lack of local SGML expertise, HTML was selected as the format.

In the summer of 2001, a new project was undertaken to convert the law cases from HTML to XML to ensure long-term preservation, to enhance their utility, and to experiment with search and retrieval systems.

PROJECT GOALS AND JUSTIFICATION

The decision to convert the HTML cases to XML was not driven by immediate user or library staff demand for increased functionality. Usage of the digital collection was steady and higher than expected. The impetus for conversion to XML came from the data library coordinator, who wanted to ensure the utility and longevity of the digital repository. The coordinator recognized that much of the expertise about the original HTML coding and knowledge was not captured in the HTML project documentation. It would be advantageous to move the collection to a more versatile and permanent format before the staff who originally coded these files retired or left the library system.

The conversion project would also serve as a test bed for future digital library projects using XML, which some members of the library staff had started to experiment with. The only official project carried out by the library involved one developer who created an Encoded Archival Description (EAD) search engine for the University Archives. This project was an ideal size for a test bed. Staff could gain expertise with XML and XML-encoded materials, and acquire the knowledge to estimate, plan, and carry out more extensive projects.

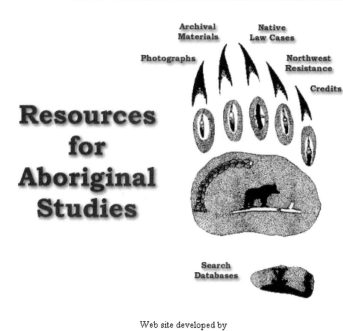

Figure 10–1. *Resources for Aboriginal Studies Web site*

Furthermore, the test bed offered an opportunity to experiment with and investigate enhanced user access to the collection. The project will be monitored to see which enhanced search capabilities are utilized and preferred by site users.

PROJECT DESCRIPTION

This project was modest in scope and size: 550 cases converted from HTML to XML, reproduced from a nine-volume set called the *Canadian Native Law Cases.* Most of the cases were in English; a small number were in French. The initial project plan and estimates indicate that conversion should be a straightforward undertaking. Much of the conversion could be automated. It was anticipated that the selection and determination of the useful semantic elements would take time, as would the development of a Document Type Definition (DTD). Any elements not coded in the original HTML version, but important for search and retrieval, would require time for manual coding.

Two permanent staff members, the data library coordinator and a programmer analyst, worked on the project for four months on a part-time basis. A student assistant was dedicated to the project 60% of the time for the four-month period. The software used for the project was either free or very inexpensive.

The collection of law cases is not as consistent as one might assume. It is a heterogeneous collection of documents published by many different courts over a period of more than 100 years. The collection presents different formatting and typography styles. The additional work of creating a DTD and providing an external record of the valid tags and hierarchical relationships was deemed useful for this XML project as an aid to conversion and manual coding work, as well as to provide an ongoing record of the structure.

The proposed work plan had the following stages:

1. Research existing case law DTD options.
2. Identify the semantic elements critical to the native law case project.
3. Evaluate the ease of mapping HTML elements to the required semantic elements.
4. Develop or adapt DTD and then validate it.
5. Parse the HTML cases.
6. Manually enhance and add new elements that could not be created by the parser.
7. Validate the XML of all cases.
8. Use XSLT and Xalan, an XSLT style sheet processor, to create XHTML versions of the case.
9. Index XML version of the cases with Inktomi search engine.
10. Study and evaluate the use of the search engine and cases.

Researching DTDs

The first area under investigation was the DTD development. Would a special DTD have to be created for this project, or could a subset of Text Encoding Initiative (TEI) or another DTD like DocBook be utilized?

The student assistant, a computer science graduate student in learning technologies, was charged with two research tasks:

- locate DTDs developed especially for law cases or legal materials, and
- evaluate the appropriateness of TEI and TEI Lite (a simplified version of TEI) for the project.

The research phase did not uncover DTDs specifically designed for law cases or any derivatives of TEI for use with law cases. The TEI element set is very extensive and robust, but the types of elements needed for law cases were not well represented. Ultimately, a custom DTD was created for the law cases, utilizing elements from TEI where appropriate. The TEI header and some of the mechanisms for coding typography were adopted and used. The TEI header makes it possible to construct title pages or provide bibliographic information about the case and volume. In the future, being able to share these elements will likely be important for collaborative digital library initiatives.

Element Set for Case Law

None of the members of the ad hoc project team had extensive experience with legal materials or case law. The expertise and insight into user needs was gained through consultation with the director of the Law Library. Cases were examined and the elements essential for information retrieval were duly noted. Reference books on legal research and the parts of cases were also examined. The goal of the project was to provide a research site that would support the work of scholars rather than that of legal practitioners. The original nine-volume set was a derivative work; legal practitioners prefer and are usually required to cite the original case law reporters.

Some of the important semantic elements identified for law cases were:

- style of cause
- year of decision
- reporter
- first page

- jurisdiction
- court
- judges

Many of the elements could have been coded at a much finer level of detail. The style of cause has nine main subelements. Given the lack of granularity in the original coding, the addition of "possible" elements was carefully weighed against the time available for manual coding. Fortunately, the finest level of granularity was not necessary for the type of use by scholarly researchers.

Mapping HTML Elements to XML

Some key strengths of the original HTML project helped with the conversion. The original project had a clearly defined set of rules for encoding parts of the case. Specific parts of the case had been identified as critical for future conversion and had been assigned unique tags or pairs of HTML tags. For example, the main statement of cause or title of the case was coded thus:

```
<H2><CENTER>Statement of Cause</CENTER></H2>
```

The combination of <H2><CENTER> tags was used only for the statement of cause. Each page break contained information on the original case's publication pagination (important for legal reference and citation) and the pagination of the particular print volume set. This information was also captured during the HTML conversion and was coded as:

```
<!—<CENTER>(437) A.G. of Canada v. FOWLDS 5</CENTER> — >
```

Many elements could be easily mapped from HTML to XML:

- statement of cause
- case reporter
- page break
- footnotes
- marginalia

- preamble
- typography

Other elements would require manual coding. Some of the elements—*caseheader, casetitle,* and *casereporter*—could automatically be parsed and tagged. Elements such as *court* could be identified by the parser, but the nested elements were coded by hand: *judge, year, jurisdiction,* and *courtname.*

This excerpt from the DTD shows some of the elements that were either converted or coded by hand.

```
<!ELEMENT caseheader (casetitle I casereporter I court I pb I para)*>
<!ELEMENT casetitle (#PCDATA I seg I footnote)*>
<!ELEMENT casereporter (#PCDATA I seg I footnote)*>
<!ELEMENT court (#PCDATA I judge I year I jurisdiction I courtnameI seg I footnote)*>
<!ELEMENT judge (#PCDATA)>
<!ELEMENT jurisdiction (#PCDATA)>
<!ELEMENT courtname (#PCDATA)>
<!ELEMENT year (#PCDATA)>
```

DTD Development

Considerable time and effort were spent developing a DTD for the cases. This process was more time-consuming than anticipated for a variety of reasons. Due to time constraints, the final DTD for the law cases was put on hold. It was imperative that the project continue to move ahead so that the manual coding could be completed during the project window. An interim DTD was quickly developed that would work with the HTML parser and allow the student to begin enhancements to the coding.

Perl Parser

The programmer analyst was able to utilize the original coding rules for the HTML cases to develop a parser, which was written in Perl. Many elements were easy to parse and identify. Overall, the programming time required for developing and refining the parser was less than a week from start to finish, including subsequent revisions.

The following excerpt shows part of the case *In Re Armour*

and the Township of Onondaga. The HTML coding has been removed and XML elements are used. The manual coding and enhancing of the court element described above have been completed.

```
<caseheader>
<casetitle>IN RE ARMOUR AND THE TOWNSHIP OF ONONDAGA</casetitle>
<casereporter>(1907), 14 O.L.R. 606 (also reported: 9 O.W.R. 833)</casereporter>
    <court>
          <jurisdiction>Ontario</jurisdiction>
<courtname>High Court</courtname>,
<judge>Riddel</judge> J., 26 April<year>1907</year>
</court>
    <para>(Motion to appeal to Supreme Court of Canada,
    reported sub nom. Armour v. Township of
    Onondaga, infra p. 9)</para>
</caseheader>
```

Manual Coding

After parsing, the cases were tested with XMLSpy to see if they were valid. The initial parse revealed that the many of the early cases coded in 1994 had instances of incorrect or inconsistent HTML. The HTML cases were edited manually and corrected, then they were run through the parser again. Fortunately, this cleanup task took only about three full-time days.

After the HTML cleanup, the simplified DTD was refined. Typographical elements such as bold and italic were removed in favor of using attributes on elements having semantic meaning, like paragraph or style of cause. Structure was added, and elements were grouped together. Some of the new elements added to the DTD required manual coding. The student edited the individual case files to code new elements like court name, jurisdiction, names of the judges, court citation, and year of the judgment.

XML Cases Generated as XHTML

Static XHTML files were batch generated from the XML files using the Xalan XSL style sheet processor and then uploaded to the Web server. The XSLT style sheet was simple and straight-forward to create. In the following XSLT code, when a casetitle, casereporter, or court tag was encountered, its contents would be tagged with the appropriate XHTML tag (<h2> or <h3>):

```
<xsl:template match="casetitle">
  <h2><xsl:apply-templates/></h2>
</xsl:template>
<xsl:template match="casereporter">
  <h3><xsl:apply-templates/></h3>
</xsl:template>
<xsl:template match="court">
  <h3><xsl:apply-templates/></h3>
</xsl:template>
```

PROBLEMS AND CHALLENGES, SUCCESSES AND FAILURES

This project, like many, had its share of surprises, both good and bad. The research into DTDs raised many thorny questions: Should a unique DTD be developed? How much should be borrowed from TEI? Then there were time management considerations: How many new elements could be coded by hand within the time frame?

On the positive side, the rigorous coding rules established with the earlier project were a great boon to this project. HTML documents that were not consistently constructed from a set of rules would have been impossible to convert in such a short time. Another advantageous factor was the nature of case law. Distinct elements occurred in a reasonably consistent fashion and could be easily identified and isolated. Although law cases were an unfamiliar document format at the start of the project, it was very easy to grasp the document structure.

On the negative side, it became obvious that creation of the DTD was slowing down the project. Continuing to work on the "perfect DTD" would delay and jeopardize the project's completion. The decision was made to switch horses in midstream and reverse engineer the HTML cases to construct a rudimentary DTD. This changed the workflow dramatically. The programmer analyst was confident that the rudimentary DTD could be refined and enhanced easily. The original plan to parse the HTML and then work directly in the XML version of the cases was set aside. Given that the DTD would be evolving, it was necessary to correct the HTML cases so that valid XML documents could be generated as the DTD was developed.

In retrospect, this detour actually proved to be the best approach for this type of project. It was immediately evident which semantic elements could be extracted from the HTML coding and which could not. The iteration of the DTD allowed new elements to be added and coded as time permitted.

Another minor hurdle was discovering that the original HTML files were not valid and contained errors. Fortunately, the cleanup did not take long, but this setback was unexpected. When programming the parser, it was difficult to decide how many errors and exceptions to check for and where to draw the line: When would manual editing be more efficient? Experimentation made it clear that programming for exceptions and missing elements was not a particularly effective strategy. The elements and cases that could be converted with 100% certainty became the main focus of attention.

PLANS

Indexing with Inktomi and On-the-Fly Conversion with AxKit

In the future, the XML law cases will be indexed with Inktomi search engine. Cases will be converted on the fly from XML to XHTML using AxKit, an XML application server for the Apache Web server. The project Web site and search engine logs will be monitored to see how new search features are utilized by researchers.

TIPS AND ADVICE (LESSONS LEARNED)

In order to create a useful and usable XML document, it is crucial to analyze and understand the native document type. It is important to identify elements that the user community particularly cares about from a semantic point of view, and to distinguish these from those that are unnecessary or rarely needed. The limited project budget forced the work team to identify the most important elements. The actual task of identifying the key elements becomes easy once the document structure and user needs are clearly understood.

Constructing a DTD is not a trivial task. Many projects would not require the development of a DTD, but for this project, it was a useful undertaking. None of the team members was familiar with encoding legal materials. It forced the project team to clearly identify the elements that would be encoded for each law case. By having a DTD, we could maintain consistency by enforcing encoding standards during the conversion process. The DTD also provides a reference point for translating from XML to other formats.

Perhaps one of the most useful findings is also the most obvious after the fact. During the DTD development, we frequently eyeballed the print cases, looking for the required elements and exceptions to our DTD. In practice, the parser was far more effective at finding exceptions and inconsistencies in the proposed DTD. With the parser, it was immediately evident if an element existed in every case and could be designated as required, or if the order was consistent and elements could be identified as sequential. The frequency with which particular elements appeared could also be determined.

IMPLICATIONS

HTML files with consistent coding and range of elements can be readily converted to XML. Two parallel processes could be considered. The programmers could begin by parsing the HTML files and mapping the HTML elements to a skeletal XML structure. At the same time, the important elements for metadata and specific searching by users could be identified, and additional manual coding could be carried out. By parsing the collection early in the project, it is easy to determine how many elements can be extracted correctly and unambiguously. This will immediately allow you to:

- determine how many elements can be parsed,
- determine the extent of manual coding involved, and
- prevent bottlenecking by allowing the programming, validation, and manual coding to work in parallel with DTD development.

Over the past seven years, many libraries digitized or coded materials in HTML, which was a quick and easy way to make materials accessible to users. With advances in the HTML standard, many of the elements once used are now deprecated, and within one or two years may no longer be supported by state-of-the-art Web browsers. As custodians of knowledge, librarians need to consider appropriate migration paths for digital content.

The native law project was an excellent test bed. It clearly demonstrates that with a modest investment of time and the use of inexpensive tools, it is possible to migrate document repositories from HTML to XML. It is essential to have a programmer parse as much of the original HTML documents as possible to speed up the conversion. Even small libraries can use XML to preserve digital content for the long haul.

CONTACTS

Darlene Fichter
Data Library Coordinator
(306) 966-7209
darlene.fichter@usask.ca
http://library.usask.ca/~fichter/

Doug MacDonald
Programmer Analyst
(306) 966-5939
doug.macdonald@usask.ca

University of Saskatchewan Library
3 Campus Drive
Saskatoon, SK Canada S7N 5A4

LINKS AND RESOURCES

AxKit
axkit.org
AxKit is an XML application server for Apache. It provides on-the-fly conversion from XML to HTML or other formats.

Inktomi
www.inktomi.com
Inktomi is a full-text search engine that has XML support.

Resources for Aboriginal Peoples
library.usask.ca/native/
This Web site includes digitized content about aboriginal people, including photographs, archival materials, and law cases.

TEI Lite
www.hcu.ox.ac.uk/TEI/Lite/
A subset of TEI, TEI Lite was based on experience encoding texts at the Oxford Text Archive and elsewhere.

Xalan
xml.apache.org/xalan-j/
Xalan (named after a rare musical instrument) provides XSLT style sheet processing. It is available in Java and in alpha for C++.

XHTML
www.w3.org/TR/xhtml1/
The Extensible HyperText Markup Language is a reformulation of HTML as XML.

XML Spy
www.xmlspy.com
XML Spy is an editor that supports XML editing and validation, schema and DTD editing, and XSL editing and validation.

11

Transforming Word Processing Documents into XML: Electronic Scholarly Publishing at the University of Michigan

Brian Rosenblum
University of Michigan

BACKGROUND

The Scholarly Publishing Office (SPO), a unit of the University Library at the University of Michigan, provides tools and methods for the electronic publication and distribution of scholarly content. The office supports the transformation of print journal and monographic publications to an online environment, as well as publishing scholarly work expressly designed for electronic delivery.

One major aspect (and major challenge) of our work, which this chapter will describe, is the data preparation process in which we transform scholarly material from the "native" format in which it was produced into Text Encoding Initiative (TEI)–based XML. This involves working directly with faculty, editors, and publishers to educate them about the production and use of XML and to provide the tools they need to help facilitate the transformation of data to XML, as well as developing our own production and conversion methods.

Because a number of the projects that SPO works on are

highly idiosyncratic (scholarly databases or extensive Web sites with significant scholarly content), this article will limit its focus to the preparation process for journal articles, which share certain characteristics across publications and about which some useful generalizations can be made.

PROJECT GOALS AND JUSTIFICATION

The goals of our project are:

- to develop low-cost scalable mechanisms for electronic publication and distribution of journals and monographs. Specifically, with regard to the data preparation process, to develop tools and processes to convert documents from various native formats to XML.
- to provide tools and templates for content providers to produce and submit articles in a way that will facilitate the transformation to XML, while allowing those providers the freedom to make independent decisions about their online publication models.
- to educate publishers about the practical uses and benefits of XML.

Journals vary widely in their production methods and in their publication models. Material comes to SPO in various formats (Quark, PageMaker, MS Word), and publishers have different requirements for their online publication models. Some publishers want to publish one article at a time, immediately after it is accepted for publication; others want online publication of an issue to coincide with or lag several months after the print publication. Some want to display the fully encoded electronic text; others want to display PDF files, using the XML only for searching. Our goal was to develop a generalizable conversion process that would be integrated smoothly into our other services (such as our Web submission and journal management system, or the DLXS digital library software), and that would allow each journal to retain its own specific publication preferences.

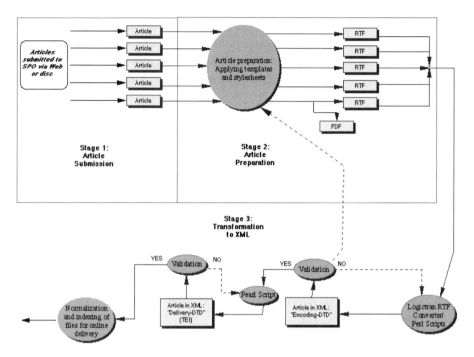

Figure 11–1. Overview of the process of transforming text from word processing documents to XML

PROJECT DESCRIPTION

In the ideal XML world, an initial master copy of an article or issue would be created in XML, and this version would be used to create all the derivative versions, both print and online. But most journals (particularly in the humanities, which has been SPO's focus) are not produced this way, for several reasons: because the tools are still not readily available, because journals have well-established production methods and are reluctant to change, and because publishing staff are still exploring what it means to publish online.

Content that is encoded in XML can be processed and made available online through DLXS, the suite of tools and search engine that provides the foundation for digital library services at the University of Michigan. The DLXS search engine, XPAT, is a powerful SGML/XML-aware tool that supports searching, indexing, and retrieval of encoded information. The DLXS "middleware" tools are designed to process and support access to various types of digital collections and various "behaviors" associated with these collections (such as different types of searches, browse, and remembering search histories).

Thus, the goal of our preparation process is to get material from the format in which it was originally created into XML. In the case of journal articles, we use a TEI-based DTD we call "textclass."[1] The journey of each article from its native format to XML can be broken down into three (sometimes overlapping) stages: submission, preparation, and transformation (outlined in Figure 11–1).

Submission

Articles are submitted by journals to SPO in a variety of formats, usually after they have been prepared for printing, and often after the print version has already been published. Articles are submitted either via the Web through an Oracle-based submission system developed by SPO, or via e-mail attachments or on CD. The Web-based system requires the content provider to enter bibliographic information about the article that is then used to create TEI headers at the time of submission. If the articles are submitted via disk after formatting by the typesetter, or by e-mail attachment, SPO will usually create a record for each article in a FileMaker database from which the TEI header will be created. These headers will be attached to the articles at a later time, either after the preparation process just before transformation to XML, or after they have been transformed to XML.

---

1. "Textclass" is one of the evolving set of "classes" supported by DLXS. These classes include:
   - text collections (page-image-based books with associated OCR, and SGML/XML-encoded books and journals)
   - bibliographic data
   - EAD-encoded finding aids
   - digital images and image metadata
   - encyclopedic reference works

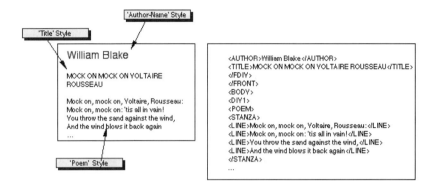

Figure 11–2. *Text in a word processing document with paragraph styles (left); the same text transformed into a tagged document (right)*

Preparation

This stage is crucial to the success of the final transformation. It is often the most time-consuming stage, and it requires the most hands-on work. In order to get a well-structured document at the end of the process, it is necessary to put a well-structured document in at the start. The goal of this stage is to create a well-structured file in Rich Text Format (RTF) that can then be transformed into XML. In this case, *well-structured* means having strictly defined paragraph and character styles applied to all the text in the document. These styles identify the structural elements of the article (for example, author, title, blockquote, epigraph), rather than layout characteristics such as bold, indent, and font size (see Figure 11–2).

Not only are articles submitted to SPO in a variety of file formats (Quark, PageMaker, Word, etc.) but the use of style sheets varies widely from journal to journal. Some publications are quite good at making use of style sheets, and we can use the files almost "as is." Other journals use them very inconsistently; we have created templates in Microsoft Word with a set of standard styles that we can provide to journal staff for their use. Articles that are processed after the print version has been created are usually the most inconsistent. Typesetters rely heavily on style sheets, but it turns out that the material we receive that has already been typeset is not always very useful for us. Because typesetters are concerned about how the text will look on the page, they will make numerous minor adjustments to the text, while our use of XML is concerned primarily about the structure of the document (what a particular section of text *is*, rather than what it will look like).

Every article that is submitted to us is prepared either by double-checking the styles created by the editor or the typesetter, or by applying our own styles from scratch to every paragraph in the article. With some practice, a 20-page article can usually be prepared in a matter of minutes.

After applying the styles to the article, the file is saved in RTF format. (Depending on the original software application used to create the article, sometimes it is easier to save as RTF first and then apply the styles.)

Transformation

Once the articles are in RTF format, we place them on a Unix server and use a combination of tools—Logictran RTF converter, Perl scripts, sp, all brought together with Unix shell scripts—to transform the files from RTF to textclass in just a few short steps. RTF converter is an affordable program that can create hierarchical XML tags based on the paragraph and style names of RTF documents. It allows the user to specify the styles and tags, and with some light programming work the user can also use string and numerical variables, and create conditional statements and functions to output a hierarchical, tagged document. For example, here is a (simplified) line of code from our conversion script:

```
'POEM', '<POEM>\n<STANZA>\n<LINE>', '</LINE>\n</STANZA>\n</POEM>', '<TAB>',
'<TAB>', "$AfterStanza()<LINE>', ' ',1,1,0,0,0,1
```

This line of code indicates how to process text that has the paragraph style 'POEM.' The line indicates what tags to place at the beginning of the text, what tags to place at the end of the text, what tags to place at each carriage return in the text, plus a number of other variables, such as whether to allow nested tags or not. '$AfterStanza' invokes a function (not shown here) that will check to see if the stanza has ended and put the appropriate tags in place.

The program can batch process entire directories, which makes it useful for transforming entire issues or runs of journals into XML. After the program is run, we also do some simple cleaning up and final transformation of the data with Perl.

While the RTF converter is good at outputting complex tagged documents, the output is not necessarily valid XML. After the output file is created, we attach the header (if it has not already been attached) and then use the Unix-based validation program sp to validate the article. In fact, we validate the text twice, because we are using two different DTDs. Textclass (or TEI) is used as a "delivery" DTD—this is the DTD that the content is stored in and delivered to the user (transformed to HTML on the fly). However, because it is very loosely structured (any element may appear almost anywhere), it is not really suitable for encoding and validation purposes. An article may be in valid textclass, but it still might not make any sense. Thus we use an intermediary "encoding" DTD, which we refer to as journal.dtd. This DTD is more strict regarding where it allows elements to appear, and is intended to ensure that a given text really does conform to the structure of a typical journal article. If we get validation errors, then we need to either fix the original RTF file or modify the DTD to handle some new element. Once the articles are validated against the journal DTD, a simple Perl transformation script can transform them to textclass, where they are again validated (see Figure 11–1, Stage 3). After the articles are validated in textclass, they are ready for normalizing, indexing, and putting online.

PROBLEMS AND CHALLENGES, SUCCESSES AND FAILURES

Multiple Processes

Not all journals are created equal. One of our main challenges has been learning how to handle material from a variety of sources, often each with its own unique characteristics, while still maintaining a relatively simple system through which all or most of the material can be processed. The material we receive comes in a variety of file formats and varies significantly from journal to journal in terms of the initial structure of the content. The peculiarities of the different native formats (such as the various ways of handling footnotes, or the use of separate "stories" or text boxes in Quark and PageMaker) sometimes make it awkward to export to RTF format. In addition, the material is submitted to us using different methods (sometimes via the Web submission system, sometimes delivered on disk). Finally, each journal has its own publication specifications. *Philosophers' Imprint* publishes one article at a time in PDF format. *Michigan Quarterly Review* makes each issue available as encoded electronic text (HTML) six months after the print version is published.

In short, because each journal may have its own unique characteristics and requirements in terms of content and production, the transformation process may differ slightly for each one. Thus we have found ourselves managing slightly different processes for each journal—for example, attaching the header (generated by a database) at different points in the process depending on how the article was submitted and who created the database record, or using TEI level 2 or level 4 markup, depending on how the material will be displayed on the Web. At the moment, as Figure 11–1 shows, we address most of these differences in the preparation phase of the process (preparing the article in its native format and saving as RTF). Once we are ready for the actual transformation of the data (Stage 3), we have a single procedure for all of the texts.

Having a separate preparation process for each journal would rapidly become unwieldy as the number of journals increases. By creating a set of standard templates for journal editors to use, we hope to standardize some of the processes across journals. We also plan to create several generalizable "classes" or categories of publications, based on their production processes and online publication models. By doing so, we will be able to manage a growing number of publications by sending them through one of a handful of processes.

Encoding DTD Often Changes

As mentioned earlier, we use an encoding DTD (journal.dtd) for validation purposes before transforming the text to the much looser textclass (TEI) DTD. The journal DTD is intended to be a much stricter DTD, which should ensure that the articles are indeed in a format that will work with our search engine and online delivery system. In reality, the journal DTD is in constant flux. This was especially true in the early days as we began to encode our first articles and develop the DTD, but it remains true to some extent as new articles that have elements not previously encountered are processed. As this new content comes in, we sometimes need to add tags to the journal DTD, or to modify it in other ways, and it becomes looser and looser until it begins to resemble TEI itself. We then need to tighten it up.

Keeping the right balance presents a challenge, and it may eventually be the case that having several encoding DTDs for different journals or for different stages in the process will be a better way to ensure strict compliance with a set of structural rules.

There is a strong need to find a balance between customization and standardization, automation and hand intervention, while taking into consideration the learning time and manpower required to run multiple processes. Finding the right balance is not always easy, and depends in large part on the capabilities of the organization and the needs and desires of the content providers.

Conversion Tools

Finding the right tools to use also took some time, because when we began there was little information about how to get material into XML in a low-cost, efficient way. We tried various software tools, including Avenue.quark, which we hoped would help us with the large amount of material that we receive in QuarkXpress format. This proved to be completely unworkable for our needs. The Logictran RTF converter was the best tool we found at the time that could batch process large amounts of material quickly; give us complex, hierarchical tagged output; be configured to work with Perl scripts and other tools; and work on Unix, Mac, or PC. It was inexpensive and provided good support, but it involved a significant learning period. It also requires some light programming skills to take full advantage of its capabilities, but it has proven to be quite powerful and suitable for our needs for the time being, especially when combined with some Perl scripts to help clean up and transform the material. We have seen a number of other tools that will get material into a flat tagged structure, which can then be modified using Perl. The advantage we find with the RTF converter is its ability to output embedded tags and to batch process, as well as its flexibility and computability with other tools such as Perl, Image Magick, Graphic Converter, and others.

Philosophers' Imprint

Philosophers' Imprint is an example of how we have successfully brought a number of elements together to create an efficient method for a new, low-cost model of electronic scholarly publishing. This electronic-only, peer-reviewed publication edited by philosophy faculty at the University of Michigan publishes articles singly, as they are accepted and prepared for publication, in PDF format, freely available on the Web. Working closely with the editors, SPO created an MS Word template with paragraph styles, which the editors use to create the document. From this original Word document, the PDF file can be created at the click of a button. And because the Word document makes use of strictly applied paragraph and character styles, the XML can also be generated almost as easily. The articles are submitted via our Web-submission system, so that the headers are automatically generated and attached to the XML file. If there are no validation errors or other unforeseen occurrences, we can have a new article published and searchable on the Web within a matter of minutes after it is submitted.

PLANS

Much of our time in 2001 was spent on experimental learning projects and on developing our tools and systems. As these first collections and publications go online, we will be able to devote time to streamlining our processes and expanding our activities. SPO is continually looking at implementing new services, such as print on demand, peer-review systems, or expanding into new forms of electronic scholarly publishing (electronic databases, multimedia presentations, etc.). As we do so, we will need to modify our data transformation activities accordingly to integrate them smoothly with our overall activities. Specifically, for the text preparation and transformation activities themselves, we have a number of areas we plan to work on.

Consolidating Scripts and Files

Our most immediate plans are to consolidate and fine-tune our processes. The largely trial-and-error method by which we developed our text transformation process has resulted in a number of discrete scripts and databases, as we have tried, discarded, and retried various methods and tools. These procedures will be revised, standardized, and documented.

Developing and Documenting Publication Models

Based on our current publications, SPO will develop a set of generalizable models that can be reemployed for other publications. This will allow us to address the different needs of content providers, and to scale up the number of our publications while still keeping a manageable system in place. Each model represents costs and benefits in terms of time, money, functionality, and visual appeal, and each has implications for the data transformation process. SPO will document each of these models in order to help content providers make informed decisions about their publication needs.

Developing and Improving Editorial Tools

We plan to work more closely with content providers to develop better tools and processes for the production of their material. This includes enhancing our Web-based article submission system (possibly developing it into a larger peer-review tracking system), integrating it more fully into the text transformation process (by improving and expanding its ability to automatically generate and attach headers and initiate the transformation process), and making it easier to use and able to handle more types of submissions (so that most material will eventually be delivered to us through this system rather than by disk or e-mail).

We also plan to develop more templates for producing texts and applying style sheets to articles. By working with content providers in this way, we also hope to educate them more about XML, the advantages of using it, and the tools needed to create it. In this way, we would eventually like to be able to push back some of the initial article preparation activities to the content providers themselves (these activities often involve editorial decisions more appropriate for them to make). This has proved successful with *Philosophers' Imprint* and, if it is successful with other journals as well, it will free up some of our own time and resources for further development and expansion of other services.

TIPS AND ADVICE (LESSONS LEARNED)

We learned several important things during our initial period of development.

- There was a significant amount of setup time in getting this system working: time spent finding the appropriate software, preparing templates, setting up the scripts, the trial-and-error method of figuring things out. In our case, however, the initial preparatory work paid off in the end because we can now process a steady stream of incoming material in a relatively quick and efficient manner. In addition, the more data preparation we can push back onto the editorial and production staff, the more we will be able to scale our operations up and handle larger amounts of material.

- Getting already existing data into XML (as opposed to creating data directly in XML) is very much a hands-on process. The bulk of the work comes from applying structure to the initial documents and, in a case like ours in which we have continuous new material coming in, monitoring the conversion output and modifying the transformation process as needed.

- Structure data early. The more structured the data going in, the more you can do with it. We spend the bulk of our time preparing data by applying styles and shaping the initial documents before doing any kind of data transformation.

- Having a constantly ongoing stream of incoming material will also necessarily result in ongoing modifications to the DTD and to the process, because one can never predict what will be in the next article. Even after processing many journal articles, we find that we need to make regular modifications to our DTDs and transformation scripts to handle new items or structures in the content.

IMPLICATIONS

While our experience has shown that there is a lot of hands-on work involved, especially in the initial setup stage, it also demonstrates that effective transformation of text to XML can be done quickly and with a small staff. (Our text transformation is done by one employee working part-time on developing and maintaining the conversion scripts, and one-part time student assistant helping to apply styles to the articles.)

The electronic journal *Philosophers' Imprint* demonstrates the value of electronic publishing: by bypassing traditional publishing houses and making the articles freely available directly to the reader via the Web, they are able to distribute the journal at virtually no cost. While the value of XML in enabling this kind of publishing has been much touted, and other chapters in this book show how to use XML to achieve this, I hope we have also shown that with the proper preparation and a few simple tools, it is possible to generate XML from your existing documents.

CONTACT

Brian Rosenblum
Scholarly Publishing Office
University of Michigan Library
301 Hatcher North
Ann Arbor, MI 48109-1205

brianlee@umich.edu
(734) 615-8519
Fax (734) 647-6897

LINKS AND RESOURCES

Digital Library Extension Service (DLXS)
www.dlxs.org
The suite of tools and search engine that provides the foundation for digital library services at the University of Michigan.

Digital Library Production Service (DLPS)
www.umdl.umich.edu
Formed in 1996 to provide infrastructure for campus digital library collections, including both access systems and digitization services. Contains links to University of Michigan digital library collections, including collections representing various DLXS classes.

Logictran
www.logictran.com
Providers of the Logictran RTF converter, a tool for converting RTF documents to a tagged format.

Michigan Quarterly Review
www.hti.umich.edu/m/mqr
Online version of this print-based journal. The "Frontlist" sec-

tion (1997-present) consists of electronic text encoded in the manner described in this paper.

Philosophers' Imprint
www.philosophersimprint.org
Electronic journal published online only, one article at a time. Articles are prepared in Microsoft Word and converted to XML for online publication.

Scholarly Publishing Office, University of Michigan
spo.umdl.umich.edu
Electronic publishing initiative of the University of Michigan library. The Web site contains information about SPO's services and tools and links to its online publications.

Text Encoding Initiative
www.tei-c.org
A long-standing effort to define text markup standards and guidelines for humanities scholars.

Application VII

USING XML FOR SYSTEMS INTEROPERABILITY

IN LIBRARIES

In a number of ways, XML is made for sharing data between systems. It is simultaneously machine-parsable and readable. You can look at it in the raw and have a prayer of understanding what it is describing, its structure, and how you may want to process it. It can be easily transformed and displayed to different specifications, and all that is required to be able to perform this magic is an understanding of the particular schema or definition being used. So it should come as no surprise that there are many initiatives that are developing interoperability standards based on XML.

CHAPTER 12

The Digital Library Federation's Metadata Encoding and Transfer Standard (METS) is one such effort, which is described in Chapter 12, "Encoding Digital Objects with METS" by Jerome McDonough, a key participant. This emerging standard for encoding digital objects may be our best hope for creating digital objects that can be shared easily between disparate systems while providing searching and display services for complex digital objects (for example, a diary that has both individual page images and transcribed text). METS, along with the emerging Metadata Object Description Schema (MODS, see www.loc.gov/standards/mods/ for more information), will likely provide an infrastructure that will take libraries beyond MARC and provide a foundation for services we have not yet imagined.

CHAPTER 13

Services are the focus of our final chapter, and it is coincidentally appropriate. Although the types of services described here are mostly services from one software application to another, the end result is better service to our users. In Chapter 13, "Integrating Systems with XML-based Web Services," Don Gourley describes how XML can be used to tie together various components of a system to create highly flexible and effective user services. This chapter shares some similar concepts with Chapter 2, "Searching and Retrieving XML Records via the Web," in that by using XML to share information between systems, our users can benefit without being aware of the underlying complexity required to create the services they use.

12

Encoding Digital Objects with METS

Jerome McDonough
New York University

BACKGROUND

The Making of America II (MOA2) project was a multiinstitution effort[1], coordinated by the Digital Library Federation, which sought to continue and extend research efforts developing best practices for the encoding of intellectual, structural, and administrative data about primary resources housed in research libraries. Two of the major contributions of the project were the authoring of a Digital Library Federation White Paper on digital library best practices and service models (Hurley, et al., 1999), and the creation of a test bed digital library adhering to the models set forth in the White Paper. The test bed focused on creating digital surrogates of primary source materials regarding transportation in America between 1869 and 1900.

One component of the MOA2 test bed was an XML Document Type Definition (DTD) for an encoding format that would encapsulate all of the descriptive, administrative, and structural metadata for a digitized object placed in the test bed. Drawing upon both the White Paper and previous work performed by

---

1. The project participants were the University of California at Berkeley Library, Cornell University Library, New York Public Library, Penn State University Library, and Stanford University Library.

the developers of Encoded Archival Description, the Text Encoding Initiative, and the Ebind project at U.C. Berkeley, the MOA2 DTD allowed the project participants to overlay structure on what would otherwise have been an undifferentiable mass of text and image files for the digital library objects. It also provided a flexible mechanism for linking the elements of the structure itself and the data files composing a digital library object to descriptive and administrative metadata.

Although the MOA2 DTD proved very useful within the course of the project, its scope was intentionally limited to providing an encoding format for a small class of primary source materials (textual materials and still photographic images). The DTD was also somewhat prescriptive in dictating the use of particular descriptive and administrative metadata element sets. As other institutions beyond the original MOA2 participants began experimenting with the MOA2 DTD, working around these design limitations became increasingly awkward. As a result of discussions regarding these problems among MOA2 project participants and other libraries that had been using the MOA2 DTD, the Digital Library Federation convened a workshop in February 2001 to try to determine whether a successor format to the MOA2 DTD should be created, and if so, what the requirements for such a format might be.

PROJECT GOALS AND JUSTIFICATION

The DLF workshop developed a small but specific list of requirements for any successor format to the MOA2 DTD. In addition to the primary requirement of providing an encoding format for digital library objects, the format must:

- support encoding of audio and video materials, as well as text and still image materials,
- allow for the use of a variety of descriptive and administrative metadata sets, preferably without sacrificing the capability to use the format to exchange documents between digital library repositories, and
- provide more sophisticated facilities for linking elements of the structure delineated in the document with the data

files composing the object, including the ability to link a portion of the structure with subsections of any text, image, audio, or video file.

Given these requirements, the decision to proceed with development of a successor XML format to the MOA2 DTD was not a given. There are a variety of efforts under way at the moment to develop data formats that might be seen as fulfilling the above requirements. The effort that most closely parallels the MOA2 approach while meeting the requirements for a successor format is probably the Synchronized Multimedia Integration Language (SMIL) being developed by the Synchronized Multimedia Working Group of the World Wide Web Consortium. SMIL is an XML format that allows developers to structure a variety of digital media, including text, images, audio, and video materials, into a coherent presentation, while also providing facilities for attaching descriptive metadata to such a presentation. As such, it meets many of the requirements discussed at the DLF workshop.

However, after some discussion at the workshop, it was felt that SMIL was both more and less than what was needed. SMIL provides an extensive set of elements for animation, control of presentation layout, and other features that did not seem necessary. Although SMIL provides a facility for embedding descriptive metadata within an object, it was somewhat lacking because it insists on the use of RDF format for embedding such metadata, it cannot effectively associate subelements of a structure with separate descriptive metadata sections, and it provides almost no facilities for expressing administrative metadata (its abilities in this regard being limited to a copyright statement on media elements).

Given these limitations of SMIL, the DLF decided that it was advisable to develop a new XML format for encoding digital library objects. Given the requirement to support multiple descriptive and administrative metadata sets, an XML schema was a more appropriate choice for defining the format than a DTD. After some discussion, an initial name of METS (Metadata Encoding and Transmission Standard) was given to the proposed format.

PROJECT DESCRIPTION

The METS schema defines a document format composed of six major sections:

- a header element for metadata regarding the METS document
- a descriptive metadata section
- an administrative metadata section
- a section to list and group content files for an object
- a section delineating the structure of the object
- a section identifying executable programs for use with the metadata within the METS document and the content files the METS document identifies

A complex series of connections can be drawn between elements in each of these sections using a variety of linking elements and XML ID/IDREF attributes to associate, for example, a portion of the structure of an object with descriptive metadata describing that structure, or a particular file with administrative metadata regarding the file's preservation or use.

The heart of a METS object is the structural map. This defines a hierarchical structure for the object that provides the basis for organizing the content files in the object for presentation to a user. The hierarchical structure is encoded as a nested series of <div> elements, where each <div> declares itself as being of a particular type. A book, for example, might be represented as a series of chapters:

```
<div TYPE='book' LABEL='The Hunting of the Snark'>
    <div TYPE='chapter' LABEL='Fit the First - The Landing'>
    </div>
    <div TYPE='chapter' LABEL='Fit the Second - The Bellman's Speech'>
    </div>
    .
    .
    .
</div>
```

Given a basic structure for an object such as this, the various digital representations of a work can then be tied to this common structure. Suppose, for example, that we have two versions of Lewis Carroll's *The Hunting of the Snark*: an XML version encoded using the Text Encoding Initiative's P4 DTD, and an audio version in WAV format. We might then have a file section within a METS document for this work as follows:

```
<fileGrp VERSDATE='2001-08-06'>
   <file ID='HS01' MIMETYPE='text/xml'>
      <flocat LOCTYPE='URL'>http://dlib.nyu.edu/snark.xml</flocat>
   </file>
</fileGrp>
<fileGrp VERSDATE='2001-05-13'>
   <file ID='HS02' MIMETYPE='audio/x-wav'>
      <flocat LOCTYPE='URL'>http://dlib.nyu.edu/snark.wav</flocat>
   </file>
</fileGrp>
```

The individual <div> elements within the structural map can then be linked to these content files using an <fptr> element, which identifies the linked file, and a subsidiary <area> element, which specifies an exact location within the linked file that corresponds with the structural element for a particular <div>. An updated version of our structural map above might then look like this:

```
<div TYPE='book' LABEL='The Hunting of the Snark'>
   <div TYPE='chapter' LABEL='Fit the First - The Landing'>
      <fptr>
         <area FILEID='HS01' BEGIN='CH1' END='CH2' BETYPE='IDREF' />
      </fptr>
      <fptr>
         <area FILEID='HS02' BEGIN='00:00:38:00' END='00:05:17:00'
BETYPE='SMPTE-NDF30' />
      </fptr>
   </div>
   <div TYPE='chapter' LABEL='Fit the Second - The Bellman's Speech'>
      <fptr>
         <area FILEID='HS01' BEGIN='CH2' END='CH3' BETYPE='IDREF' />
      </fptr>
      <fptr>
         <area FILEID='HS02' BEGIN='00:05:18:00' END='00:11:49:00'
```

```
BETYPE='SMPTE-NDF30' />
    </fptr>
  </div>
  .
  .
  .
</div>
```

While the compactness of the notation makes this a some-what confusing example at first glance, the structure it encodes is relatively straightforward. For the <div> representing the first chapter, we have two different content representations, signi-fied by the two <fptr> elements. The first is contained within the file in the file group section that has the XML ID value of HS01 (our TEI file), and the second in the section with the ID value of HS02 (the WAV file). Both files contain more content than just the first chapter, so each <fptr> tag contains an <area> element to specify the section of the file containing the content for the first chapter. In the case of the TEI file, we specify (us-ing the BETYPE attribute) that we are using IDREF values to specify beginning and ending locations within the referenced file; the begin point is the tag containing the XML ID attribute with the value 'CH1'. The end point is the tag with the ID value of 'CH2'. For the audio file, we use SMPTE time codes to rep-resent the start and end points; for Chapter 1, the start may be found 38 seconds into the file, and the end at 5 minutes, 17 sec-onds.

The elements within the structural map may be linked to both descriptive and administrative sections elsewhere in the METS document; files within the file group section may also be linked to administrative metadata. Unlike the structural map and file group sections of the METS schema, however, the de-scriptive and administrative metadata sections do not contain a well-defined set of elements for expressing metadata. Instead, it was decided by the group designing METS that organizations might want to have some flexibility in making their own deter-mination as to what descriptive and administrative metadata sets they might want to use. Therefore, the descriptive and ad-ministrative sections of METS are effectively defined as empty buckets, to be filled by XML data conforming to an XML schema other than METS. METS provides five different "buckets" for this purpose:

- dmdSec (descriptive metadata section)
- techMD (technical metadata regarding files and their creation)
- rightsMD (intellectual property rights metadata)
- sourceMD (descriptive and administrative metadata regarding the source material, if any, used to create the METS object)
- digiprovMD (digital provenance metadata, including information about master/derivative file relationships, file migration relations and processes)

The METS schema does provide some suggestions for organizations or individuals creating METS documents as to what additional schema they might want to use to fill in those buckets. While metadata conforming to any XML schema can be placed within these buckets, the metadata container elements in the list above allow the user to identify the type of metadata within the container, and the METS schema includes a list of metadata types that it is anticipated will be in common use for digital library objects:

- MARC (MARC21 data)
- EAD (Encoded Archival Description)
- VRA (Visual Resource Association Core Categories)
- DC (Dublin Core)
- NISOIMG (NISO Technical Metadata for Digital Still Images)
- LC-AV (Library of Congress Audio and Video Technical Metadata)
- TEIHDR (Text Encoding Initiative Header)
- DDI (Data Documentation Initiative)
- FGDC (Federal Geographic Data Committee Content Standard for Digital Geospatial Metadata)

This practice of allowing any metadata schema, while encouraging the use of a particular schema, attempts to balance the needs of organizations that require flexibility in which schema they adopt, and programmers, who need to constrain the set of possible metadata types their code must work with if tools for working with METS documents are to be practical to produce.

In addition to defining the structure, content, and descriptive and administrative metadata for a digital library object, the METS format also allows encoders to identify executable programs/behaviors that may be used in conjunction with the rest of the information in the METS document. This information is contained within the behaviors section of a METS document. For any behavior, the METS document can both identify an interface definition for the behavior and provide a link to the executable module for that behavior. This allows the METS format to support the object-oriented paradigm more completely, providing a single document that can identify all of the behaviors, content, structure, and metadata needed to make use of the digital library object.

PROBLEMS AND CHALLENGES, SUCCESSES AND FAILURES

METS is still in the early stages of its development, and there are a variety of issues that must be confronted before it can be easily adopted and used by those preparing libraries of digital content. The two greatest challenges facing METS at this point are primarily organizational in nature, and not technical. The first is the need to develop an organizational structure for registering sets of values for use within METS attributes (such as METS object type, metadata type, and location type information), and for registering XML extension schemata to use in conjunction with METS for encoding descriptive and administrative metadata. The second is the need to coordinate the development of readily available tools for creating and displaying METS objects.

Probably the greatest success of the METS work to date is simply bringing together a large number of concerned parties within the library community to try to develop a workable solution to the problem of encoding descriptive, administrative, and structural metadata. The rapid development of the METS schema can be taken as a sign of the vitality and cooperative spirit of the community trying to build up libraries of digital content.

PLANS

Version 1.0 of the METS schema has just been completed and will be reviewed by the members of the Digital Library Federation. Following that review, participants in the METS initiative will further review and develop the schema, and will confer on how to set up registry systems for recording extension schemas and type lists for use in METS documents. Finally, several organizations participating in the METS initiative are planning on collaborating on tool development, and possibly on creating a test bed of METS objects/tools for further experimentation.

IMPLICATIONS

The METS format was developed primarily because existing or proposed document encoding formats did not appear adequate to support libraries' need to capture and maintain complex and comprehensive metadata regarding objects encoded using those formats. However, there are document formats that attempt to address some of the same structural metadata issues that METS addresses, including both SMIL and MPEG-7. Because these alternative formats enjoy significant commercial support, it is likely that a variety of software tools to support them will be more readily available than for METS. If the library community at large commits to METS as a document standard, it is also committing itself to a group effort to develop tools for processing METS documents. Participants in the METS initiative are working on tool development, but it is worth nothing that SMIL tools are already in commercial use in such products as RealServer/Player. If METS is to succeed as a community standard, the library community must start sharing the burden of software development and engaging in significant collaboration and coordination to maximize the limited development resources available to libraries.

There are benefits to this approach beyond just the existence of METS as a document exchange format, however. Through the METS initiative, some of the major libraries engaged in digital library development efforts have already started trying to co-ordinate their work with regards to formalizing administrative and descriptive metadata sets for use in digital libraries. We have also taken significant steps toward collaborating in development of digital library tools that would have been difficult to achieve a few years ago. In this way, METS is realizing one of the goals identified in the Making of America II White Paper: by agreeing on standards for digital library objects, libraries find themselves in a far better position to start sharing development of new services within digital libraries. Further development of both the METS format and related efforts represents a real opportunity for digital library developers to move forward in providing new and innovative services to the communities we serve.

CONTACT

Jerome P. McDonough
Digital Library Development Team Leader
Elmer Bobst Library, New York University
70 Washington Square South
New York, NY 10012
(212) 998-2425
jerome.mcdonough@nyu.edu

LINKS AND RESOURCES

Data Documentation Initiative
www.icpsr.umich.edu/DDI/
The Data Documentation Initiative is an effort, hosted by the Inter-University Consortium for Political and Social Research, to develop an XML encoding format for code books describing data sets in the social and behaviorial sciences. The DDI format provides extensive descriptive metadata regarding data sets and is an obvious choice to use in conjunction with METS for describing data sets.

Digital Library Federation
www.diglib.org
The Digital Library Federation sponsored the Making of America II project, which preceded the METS Initiative, as well as launching the METS Initiative itself.

Dublin Core
www.dublincore.org
The Dublin Core Metadata Initiative is an open forum seeking to develop a basic descriptive metadata element set for use in a variety of applications. It provides a basic set of elements for describing parts or the entirety of a METS object.

The Ebind Project
sunsite.berkeley.edu/Ebind/
Developed by Alvin Pollock and Daniel Pitti, the Ebind project was one of the earliest efforts within the library community to provide structural metadata regarding digital library objects within an SGML encoding format. As such, it can be considered the ancestor of such work as the MOA2 DTD and the METS schema.

Encoded Archival Description
lcweb.loc.gov/ead/
Maintained by the Network Development and MARC Standards Office of the Library of Congress in conjunction with the Society of American Archivists, the EAD provides a standardized encoding format for machine-readable archival finding aids.

Federal Geographic Data Committee Content Standard for Digital Geospatial Metadata (CSDGM)
www.fgdc.gov/metadata/contstan.html
The CSDGM seeks "to provide a common set of terminology and definitions for the documentation of digital geospatial data." A draft XML encoding standard for CSDGM information is available, and can be used in conjunction with METS to provide geographic descriptive metadata regarding an object.

Hurley, B. J., J. Price-Wilkin, M. Proffitt, and H. Besser. 1999. *The Making of America II Testbed Project: A Digital Library Service Model.* Washington, D.C.: Council on Library and Information Resources.
www.clir.org/pubs/abstract/pub87abst.html
This report from CLIR describes the service model used in the Making of America II project as well as the metadata model underlying the MOA2 DTD, the METS schema's predecessor.

Library of Congress Audio and Video Technical Metadata Extension Schemas
lcweb.loc.gov/rr/mopic/avprot/metsmenu.html
Originally a separate effort, the Library of Congress (which is serving as the maintenance agency for the METS initiative) has developed XML schemas for technical metadata regarding audio and video files specifically for use with METS objects. This page also provides links to other METS extension schemas under development by the Library of Congress.

The Making of America II
sunsite.berkeley.edu/moa2/
The Making of America II was a Digital Library Federation project intended to investigate issues around the development of a distributed digital library of archival materials. The MOA2 DTD, developed for the project, is the predecessor format to the METS schema.

METS
www.loc.gov/standards/mets/
The official Web site for the METS initiative of the Digital Library Federation, hosted by the Network Development and MARC Standards Office of the Library of Congress.

MPEG-7
ipsi.fhg.de/delite/Projects/MPEG7/
The Web site for the MPEG-7 standard, an ISO standard for encoding of complex multimedia objects.

NISO Technical Metadata for Digital Still Images
www.niso.org/commitau.html
A draft standard under development by NISO, the data dictionary for this effort provides a comprehensive set of elements for describing the technical aspects of digital still images. Although an official XML encoding is not yet available, those seeking to embed technical metadata for still images within a METS document might wish to consider using this standard as a model for their work.

Synchronized Multimedia Integration Language
www.w3.org/AudioVideo/
A recommendation of the World Wide Web Consortium, SMIL provides an XML format for encoding structural metadata for multimedia display over the Web, as well as providing some limited facilities for encoding descriptive metadata. The METS schema's approach to structural metadata was strongly influenced by the SMIL recommendation.

The Text Encoding Initiative Consortium
www.tei-c.org/
The Text Encoding Initiative is an international project developing guidelines for the encoding of textual materials for research purposes. The TEI guidelines represent a de facto standard for encoding textual materials in the academic community, and will typically be the best choice for an encoding format for primary source materials to be used in conjunction with METS.

USMARC Standards
lcweb.loc.gov/marc/
USMARC is the standard for exchange of bibliographic information within the library community. As such, it provides one of the key descriptive metadata formats for use in conjunction with METS. An XML DTD for the format is available through the above link.

Visual Resources Association Core Categories
www.gsd.harvard.edu/~staffaw3/vra/vracore3.htm
The VRA Core Categories are a metadata set for the description
of "works of visual culture as well as the images that document
them." The categories contain a mix of descriptive and administrative metadata regarding images, and can be seen as a
complement to the NISO Technical Metadata for Digital Still
Images.

XML Schema
www.w3.org/XML/Schema/
The Web page for the XML schema language developed by the
World Wide Web Consortium. METS employs XML schema as
its defining format.

13

Integrating Systems with XML-based Web Services

Don Gourley
Washington Research Library Consortium

BACKGROUND

When considering XML for use in library applications, one often thinks of document markup and metadata encoding. Standardization and portability ensure that these XML-based library resources will continue to be usable as library applications and systems evolve. In perhaps less obvious ways, this platform independence also makes XML useful for systems integration and interoperability: distributed applications can more easily exchange data with one another if they have a standard message format that is portable across various operating system environments. Libraries often want different Web applications to work together to provide integrated services to their patrons, and XML messaging provides a means for these applications to request and receive data from each other.

This is the fundamental idea behind the emerging technologies collectively referred to as "Web services": applications communicate with each other by sending XML-encoded messages over standard Web network protocols. Web services promise to provide a new model for systems integration, with applications dynamically discovering and using different services when they run. While we wait to see if this potential is realized, the tools and protocols being developed and leveraged for Web services can be used today to help integrate library Web applications. At the Washington Research Library Consortium (WRLC) we are using these XML-based technologies to exchange information between various digital library and Web portal applications.

PROJECT GOALS AND JUSTIFICATION

ALADIN (Access to Library and Database Information Network) is the digital library system of the WRLC. It provides content and services for seven medium-size academic research libraries, including more than 500 subscription databases, digital collections (images, audio, and metadata), and library catalogs. Like many real-world digital libraries, ALADIN is built from a variety of loosely coupled commercial, open-source, and homegrown components. Integrating these disparate applications into a cohesive system has been an ongoing challenge. To simplify systems integration, we developed a middleware layer of Web services to provide uniform interfaces to distributed components of ALADIN.

The goals for the ALADIN middleware include:

- providing simple, network-accessible interfaces to shared ALADIN services and
- making ALADIN patron information available to other applications.

Traditional tools and technologies for exchanging data between distributed application components are either crude (e.g., batch file transfer) or highly complex and platform dependent (e.g., CORBA or DCOM). These technologies require low-level integration of components resulting in tightly coupled systems that are very interdependent and difficult to maintain. To avoid these problems, the ALADIN middleware layer is based on a Web services architecture using standard XML messages sent over HTTP, the ubiquitous Web network transport protocol. Open-source tools from the Apache Foundation and others provide the infrastructure, while our efforts focus on systems integration at the application level.

PROJECT DESCRIPTION

Three ALADIN application interfaces are exposed as Web services that can be accessed by Web applications or components:

- Directory Lookup Service
- Document Delivery Integration Service
- Patron Information Service

The Web services are simple Java classes that serve as front ends or wrappers around existing applications and functions to provide the appropriate interface for Web access. They leverage various toolkits and class libraries to handle the HTTP communication and XML message formatting, including serialization (creating an XML representation of application data) and deserialization (instantiating application data from an XML representation).

Directory Lookup Service

To support a consortium of universities, ALADIN must have a flexible authentication service capable of searching multiple directories. Patrons must be able to login explicitly with different kinds of identifiers (library bar code, institution ID, social security number) and implicitly based on their on-campus IP address. Several ALADIN components need to know the identity or institutional affiliation of users, including the main menu system and a personal portal (both written in Java) and a telnet-based menu for ASCII terminals (written in Perl). The directory lookup service isolates these ALADIN components from authentication changes such as new campus IP networks or student directories by receiving generic LDAP-like lookup requests and translating them into the appropriate query format for a directory (e.g., SQL to search the patron tables in our library automation system).

The current industry standard for XML messaging is the Simple Object Access Protocol (SOAP). SOAP provides a mechanism for calling remote procedures regardless of what languages the service requester and provider are written in or what platforms they run on, which makes it suitable for the di-

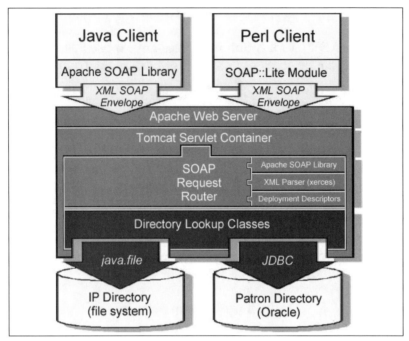

Figure 13–1. Web services architecture for the directory lookup service

rectory lookup service. The protocol consists of three parts: an envelope that encapsulates a SOAP message, XML encoding rules for serialization/deserialization, and a mechanism for invoking remote procedures. However, by using the SOAP toolkit from the Apache XML project, which takes care of the XML encoding and networking, we did not have to deal with the protocol details directly. The toolkit includes a Java client library for invoking SOAP services over the network, and a service request router that is written as a Java servlet and can load Java classes or execute scripts to provide specific services. As a Java servlet, the SOAP request router needs a JSDK-compliant servlet container in which to run, such as Tomcat from the Apache Jakarta project.

The Java classes that implement SOAP services are ordinary classes with no SOAP-specific code in them. Their public methods can be exposed through SOAP by defining them in deployment descriptors for the request router. Apache SOAP includes an administrative module that can be used to specify the deployment descriptor attributes, including class and method names, scope (whether a new class is instantiated for each request or reused), and any special classes for translating Java data structures into XML.

On the client side, accessing the directory lookup service simply involves specifying the Web service, the request router, and the method to be called. The response either will indicate some kind of error occurred or will include the attributes retrieved from the directory lookup. The following code uses the Apache SOAP *Call* class to invoke an IP address lookup:

```
URL u = new URL("http://example.wrlc.org/soap/servlet/rpcrouter");
Call call = new Call();
call.setTargetObjectURI("urn:OrgDirectory");
call.setMethodName("directoryLookup");
Vector v = new Vector();
v.addElement(new Parameter("q", String.class, "ip=192.24.36.2", null));
call.setParams(v);
Response r = call.invoke(url, "");
String result;
if (r.generatedFault())
result = r.getFault().toString()
else
        result = (String)r.getReturnValue().getValue();
```

The Perl SOAP::Lite module provides a simple way for our Perl scripts to access the directory lookup services. Here is the same SOAP call using the SOAP::Lite client library:

```
$request = SOAP::Lite
->uri('urn:OrgDirectory')
->proxy('http://example.wrlc.org/soap/servlet/rpcrouter')
->directoryLookup('ip=192.24.36.2');
if ($request->fault) {
    $result = $request->faultstring;
} else {
    $result = $request->result;
}
```

Apache SOAP Admin

Deployed Service Information

List

Deploy

Un-deploy

'urn:Prospero' Service Deployment Descriptor	
Property	Details
ID	urn:Prospero
Scope	Application
Provider Type	java
Provider Class	ORG.wlrc.services.ProsperoServer
Use Static Class	false
Methods	numDocs, updNewUser, updExistingUser
Type Mappings	
Default Mapping Registry Class	

Figure 13–2. Prospero service deployment descriptor in the Apache SOAP Admin module

Document Delivery Integration Service

Patrons can request articles from print journals via the online catalog in ALADIN. The Prospero application is used to deliver the scanned articles via the Web. Prospero is designed as a stand-alone delivery system with its own user file and login ID and password. It uses the patron's e-mail address internally to associate patrons and documents. An integration service is used to synchronize user information (like e-mail address) between ALADIN and Prospero so patrons can request and access those documents through the ALADIN portal.

This service also uses SOAP to expose its methods for re-mote execution. In this case the Web service passes data both ways: the *updNewUser* and *updExistingUser* methods add or change patron information in the Prospero user and manifest files, and the *numDocs* method reads the manifest file to provide summary information about available documents for the ALADIN patron portal. Together, these methods provide a net-work-accessible interface for sharing patron information be-tween the two distinct applications. The ALADIN components that manage that data are not affected by changes or upgrades to the Web document delivery system.

Figure 13–2 shows the Apache SOAP deployment descriptor for the document delivery integration service. It uses *application* scope so the class isn't instantiated for each request, and the methods that write to the Prospero configuration files are synchronized, guaranteeing that only one execution thread at a time will update a file. As with the directory lookup services, no special type mappings are set, so Apache SOAP will use the default methods for translating Java data types to XML.

Patron Information Service

Patron account information, such as items checked out, fines or fees due, and status of hold and recall requests, are available from the online catalog in ALADIN. Initially this information was just displayed in ALADIN on a patron's customized homepage. But as member institutions develop campus portals to consolidate access to various academic services, we need to be able to provide the information to applications as well as directly to patrons. The patron information service is designed to format data differently depending on who is requesting it.

The initial external target for the patron information service is a campus portal at American University. The Web application is written in Cold Fusion and receives data from other sources using the Web Distributed Data Exchange (WDDX) format. WDDX is simply an XML document type for expressing structured application data. Service requests are sent as standard HTTP *Get* or *Post* requests, and the HTTP response body is formatted as an XML document. Modules for serialization and deserialization of WDDX data exist for several languages besides Cold Fusion, including Java and Perl. But because this information from ALADIN was already being provided directly to browsers, we found it easier just to change the markup tags from HTML to XML in order to send it to the campus portal.

The homegrown parts of ALADIN use FreeMarker to build Web pages. FreeMarker is an open-source Java class library that generates dynamic Web pages. Instead of generating HTML strings in our Java code, we encapsulate the HTML in templates. These are compiled automatically into *template* objects, which generate HTML dynamically using data provided by our

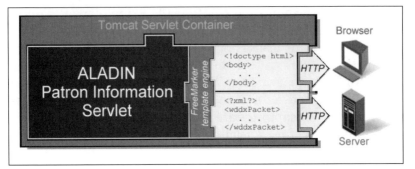

Figure 13-3. *XML and HTML template processing in the patron information service*

servlets. The template includes the formatting markup along with instructions for including data. FreeMarker instructions are simple and intuitive, but powerful enough to handle data structures of arbitrary complexity. They are also completely independent of the kind of markup used for formatting, and we found FreeMarker works as well with XML as it does with HTML. We provide patron information to the campus portal by simply creating a new template and a flag to tell ALADIN whether to use the HTML or XML template.

PROBLEMS AND CHALLENGES, SUCCESSES AND FAILURES

Performance

Performance is always a concern when extra application layers are inserted into a system, and ALADIN's middleware adds another layer to an already multitiered process. For example, when a patron logs in to ALADIN, the processing may occur on four servers: the HTTP request is received on an Apache Web server; the Tomcat module directs the request to a Java application server that is running Tomcat; the servlet calls the SOAP lookup service to retrieve the patron's attributes; and the lookup service sends an SQL query to the Oracle database server to find the patron in the library automation system.

We introduced several optimizations to try to minimize the middleware overhead. For example, we use the *application* scope for our SOAP services, which means that the Java class that provides the service is loaded and a service object is instantiated for the first request and then reused, avoiding the high overhead required in Java for object creation for each subsequent request. Also, the application server cluster is connected to the Web server via a dedicated Gigabit Ethernet link, and all servers used for ALADIN are connected to a switched 100Mb backbone, reducing network latency for the server-to-server communication. For the directory lookup service, we implemented a persistent cache in the service to hold lookup results. Subsequent lookups retrieve the response from cache until the patron's record expires or is modified in the Oracle database. Logins are faster than they were before the directory lookup service was deployed (when a separate Oracle query was performed by the application server for each login).

However, these optimizations were not as successful with the Prospero integration service. Although that service also uses the *application* scope, multiple threads cannot execute through it concurrently because they have to take turns writing to the Prospero configuration files. The Prospero integration is accomplished through the configuration files, therefore we can't avoid the inherent inefficiency of standard file system operations. Until and unless Prospero moves to a more efficient database mechanism for its user and manifest data, updating that information from ALADIN will be a relatively slow operation. Fortunately, updating the Prospero files occurs much less frequently than system logins.

Cross-platform Data Structures

We use both Java and Perl extensively in our homegrown applications, so the cross-platform portability of XML in general and SOAP in particular was very appealing to us. Overall, we found accessing Java services from Perl to be straightforward and easy. However, we did run into some problems figuring out how more complex data structures mapped between the languages. The results of a patron lookup operation are a set of attributes, each with a name and zero or more values. In Java we used a *HashMap* of arrays to represent this structure, which

SOAP encoded in XML as in this abbreviated example (with just two attributes):

```
<?xml version='1.0' encoding='UTF-8'?>
<SOAP-ENV:Envelope
xmlns:SOAP-ENV="http://schemas.xmlsoap.org/soap/envelope/"
xmlns:xsi="http://www.w3.org/1999/XMLSchema-instance"
xmlns:xsd="http://www.w3.org/1999/XMLSchema">
 <SOAP-ENV:Body>
    <ns1:directoryLookupResponse xmlns:ns1="urn:PersonDirectory"
SOAP-ENV:encodingStyle=
"http://schemas.xmlsoap.org/soap/encoding/">
    <return xmlns:ns2="http://xml.apache.org/xml-soap"
xsi:type="ns2:Map">
        <item>
        <key xsi:type="xsd:string">eduPersonOrgDN</key>
        <value xmlns:ns3="http://schemas.xmlsoap.org/soap/encoding/"
xsi:type="ns3:Array" ns3:arrayType="xsd:string[1]">
            <item xsi:type="xsd:string">WRLC</item>
        </value>
    </item>
    <item>
        <key xsi:type="xsd:string">displayName</key>
        <value xmlns:ns4="http://schemas.xmlsoap.org/soap/encoding/"
xsi:type="ns4:Array" ns10:arrayType="xsd:string[1]">
                <item xsi:type="xsd:string">Don Gourley</item>
            </value>
        </item>
    </return>
    </ns1:directoryLookupResponse>
  </SOAP-ENV:Body>
</SOAP-ENV:Envelope>
```

Java clients can simply cast the value returned by the *Response.getReturnValue().getValue()* method to any class that implements the *Map* interface to get at the attribute values. But our initial attempts to treat the result returned by the SOAP::Lite module's remote procedure call as a similar hash of arrays in Perl did not work. It turns out that the deserialization for Perl results in a reference to a hash of array references. Accessing the values requires that the data structures be dereferenced, as in this example Perl code:

```
%map = %{$request->result};
@names = @{$map{'displayName'}};
$primaryDisplayName = $names[0];
@orgs = @{$map{' eduPersonOrgDN'}};
$primaryInstitution = $orgs[0];
```

With this information, figuring out how to map complex Java data structures to their Perl equivalent is a straightforward procedure. For additional help, the SOAP::Lite package has a *+trace* flag that can be used to display the serialized XML data (like that shown above for this example) for a language-independent view of the data structure.

Authentication and User Sessions

A common challenge when exchanging user information between two Web applications is sharing authentication data so a user does not have to login separately to the two systems. Most Web application development tools provide some mechanism to identify a user across multiple page requests and to store information about that user. For example, Tomcat implements the *HttpSession* class to create a session between an HTTP client and an HTTP server. A unique identifier is assigned to each session when it is created, and Tomcat will either store that identifier in a cookie on the browser or attach it to URLs so a user is connected with that session for subsequent requests.

But when another application, such as the American University portal, is requesting the patron information, the application is identified as the client rather than the patrons who are actually seeing their account information. The external application must provide some unique credentials that identify its request as pertaining to an individual user, and the patron information service must not confuse that request with a previously created session for the external application. Fortunately, ALADIN and the AU portal both have access to the institution ID that is assigned to each member of the American University community. That ID is passed to ALADIN for each patron information request, and ALADIN will use that to create a new session even if Tomcat binds the request to a previously created session.

The patron information service also provides links back to ALADIN to perform functions, such as online renewal of borrowed items, that must be executed locally. When these links are accessed by the patron in the external application, the request is now coming from the browser rather than from the application. To transfer the session binding from the external application to the patron, the patron information service makes those links absolute (i.e., it includes the host name and full path of the URL rather than making the link relative to the current ALADIN page) and uses the *HttpServletResponse.encodeURL()* method, which tells Tomcat to add the session identifier to the URL even if the user has not disabled cookies. When using one of these links to jump from the AU portal to ALADIN, the patron is bound to the session created by the portal and does not need to login again to access the ALADIN services. The absolute encoded links also work on ALADIN pages, so no special code is required to generate them for one format or the other.

PLANS

Apache Authentication Module

The directory lookup service has proven to be a very useful abstraction for authenticating users. The use of a common interface has allowed us to make changes and performance enhancements to the directories without affecting ALADIN components. We would like to realize these benefits for a variety of other special-purpose Web sites and applications. To avoid having to create custom client code for each site (some of which are simply static collections of pages), we plan to write an Apache authentication module that could be loaded into any Apache Web server and configured in directory-specific *.htaccess* files. Using SOAP::Lite and mod_perl, we hope to create a module that would let the Web server use the directory lookup service to make sure site users are identified and properly affiliated.

Targeting Application Data for Alternative Browser Devices

By separating the data formatting from the application logic, we were able to retarget patron information to an external portal application with minimal changes to ALADIN. Because our template engine works equally well with different XML document types, it seems we could adapt ALADIN for wireless devices like PDAs by creating XML templates in the Wireless Markup Language (WML). In practice, this is likely to be more complicated because there is a somewhat different document model for WML than for HTML. In particular, handling new structural elements (like *wml:card*) and user agent processing would probably require changes to the application code. If the demand for access to ALADIN via these kinds of devices increases, we will be investigating this in more detail.

TIPS AND ADVICE (LESSONS LEARNED)

Integrating distributed applications is difficult. Using XML-based data exchange greatly simplified this task in ALADIN. XML is an open, standard mechanism for describing data structures, so we were able to find many freely available tools for processing XML messages. This allowed us to focus on the application-level data and let the tools take care of building XML messages, transporting them across the network, and processing them on different platforms.

Because XML is not tied to a particular vendor or operating system, there are many choices for supporting tools. We use mostly Java tools because that is what we are most familiar and comfortable with. But similar XML messaging toolkits exist for Perl, PHP, Cold Fusion, and Microsoft programming languages, among others. Our advice is to select the tools that provide the maximum infrastructure and functionality that can be leveraged in your environment.

IMPLICATIONS

Despite some drawbacks (such as the performance issues discussed here and a potential increase in complexity) a middleware layer provides tremendous advantages. Client components interface with a standard XML-based target (e.g., SOAP) rather than specific platforms on which services run. Those services, including their databases, programs, and configuration files, can be updated transparently, avoiding additional maintenance for each client.

This benefit is realized in the ongoing maintenance of ALADIN. For example, if we are given real-time access to a member institution's campus directory, we can modify the directory lookup service to search that directory instead or in addition to our library automation system. All components and applications that use the service will automatically get the benefit of the additional directory source. Similarly, we can enhance or replace Prospero for document delivery in ALADIN without making any changes to the various components that depend on it. By abstracting core ALADIN services to a standard XML-based interface, we can more easily add or change components of the digital library.

CONTACT

Don Gourley
Director of Information Technology
Washington Research Library Consortium
901 Commerce Drive
Upper Marlboro, MD 21401
(301) 390-2000
gourley@wrlc.org

LINKS AND RESOURCES

ALADIN
www.aladin.wrlc.org
A shared electronic library system serving American University, the Catholic University of America, Gallaudet University, George Mason University, the George Washington University, Marymount University, and the University of the District of Columbia.

Apache SOAP
xml.apache.org/soap/
An open-source Java implementation of the SOAP version 1.1 specification. Tools include a client library to invoke SOAP ser-

vices available elsewhere and server-side classes to implement SOAP-accessible services. This site also has links to more general SOAP and Web services information.

Tomcat
jakarta.apache.org/tomcat/
An open-source implementation of the current Java servlet specification. The Tomcat servlet container can be used to run the Apache SOAP request router.

SOAP::Lite for Perl
www.soaplite.com
A collection of Perl modules for deploying and accessing Web services via SOAP. This site also has links to many other SOAP toolkits and documentation.

Web Distributed Data Exchange (WDDX)
www.openwddx.org
Software development kits and documentation for XML messaging based on the WDDX DTD.

FreeMarker
freemarker.sourceforge.net
An open-source HTML and XML template engine for Java servlets.

Prospero
bones.med.ohio-state.edu/prospero/
An open-source electronic document delivery system, designed to complement to RLG's Ariel ILL system by converting Ariel documents to PDF and making them available via the Web.

Index

Page numbers in **bold** represent the primary reference.

About the Contributors

Kyle Banerjee

Kyle Banerjee is currently a systems analyst at the Oregon State Library. He previously worked at Oregon State University, where he managed a monographs processing unit in the main library. Kyle has authored several articles and delivered numerous presentations about metadata, cataloging, and automation in libraries. He received his M.L.I.S. from the University of Illinois at Urbana in 1996, and he also holds an M.A. in political science. In his spare time, Kyle enjoys cycling, playing violin, and brewing beer.

Geoff Cannon

Geoff Cannon graduated from the University of Toronto M.L.S. program in 1990. For the past 12 years he has worked for the Halton Hills Public Library, where he is currently the manager of Information Services. In recent years he has been part of a team that has migrated more than 20 electronic databases to the World Wide Web. Mr. Cannon maintains several Web sites, including the award-winning Ontario GenWeb page for Halton County.

Kevin S. Clarke

Kevin S. Clarke is the digital information systems developer at Lane Medical Library, Stanford University Medical Center. A new-school librarian/programmer, he has worked in both cataloging and information systems. Clarke graduated from UNC Chapel Hill's School of Information and Library Science in 2000. Before this, he worked in the law, rare book, and main campus libraries at UNC. Since graduation, Kevin Clarke has worked at Lane, promoting the use of XML and open-source software in the library environment.

Darlene Fichter

Darlene Fichter is a half-time data library coordinator at the University of Saskatchewan Libraries. As a data coordinator, Darlene has initiated and acted as project manager for six digital projects, mounting archival materials, law cases, photographs, articles, and indexes.

Darlene has a B.A. from the University of Saskatchewan (1981), a Teaching Certificate from the University of Saskatchewan (1982), and an M.L.S from the University of Toronto (1987). She has worked in public, academic, and special libraries, and as a library consultant.

Don Gourley

As director of information technology for the Washington Research Library Consortium, Don Gourley manages computer and network systems for a group of seven academic research libraries in the Washington, D.C., area. He designed the current version of the consortium's shared digital library system, ALADIN (Access to Library and Database Information Network).

Prior to WRLC, Don managed software projects and IT services at the Smithsonian Institution and the University of Maryland. He has published and presented on the subjects of digital libraries, information retrieval in library systems, middleware services, and open-source software.

Don holds a master's degree in computer science from the University of Colorado and a B.A. in mathematics from the University of Virginia.

Jan Lavelle

Jan Lavelle is systems librarian for Service Tasmania Online, State Library of Tasmania. Jan has a B.Sc. in Zoology from Monash University, Melbourne, Australia, and a Graduate Diploma in Librarianship from Royal Melbourne Institute of Technology. She has worked in a variety of areas in the State Library of Tasmania since 1975, including cataloging, bookmobile, reference, heritage, and library systems. She has also owned and operated a small business in the transport industry. Jan has worked on Service Tasmania Online since 1999, and was involved in the design and implementation of the XML-based application that underpins this service. She has also been involved in extending the use of XML into several other Web-based services within the State Library, including an images database, youth portal, and a public-access Internet resources guide.

Walter Lewis

Walter Lewis has served the Halton Hills Public Library for the last 20 years. He is currently manager of support services and is also responsible for the HALINET Web site and the library's information consulting services. The Community Information and Volunteer Centre software and the Newspaper Index and Genealogical databases developed by Mr. Lewis have won awards in the last two years.

Jerome McDonough

Jerome McDonough is team leader for the Digital Library Development unit at New York University. A graduate of the University of California at Berkeley School of Library and Information Studies, where he worked on such projects as the Cheshire II information retrieval system and the Making of America II project, Dr. McDonough is currently serving as chair of the editorial board for the METS initiative.

Leslie Myrick

Leslie Myrick is an application developer and database administrator on the Digital Library Team at NYU. She is currently developing XSLT style sheets for dynamic delivery of EAD-encoded finding aids, and an ingest database and search engine to enhance access to the New York Historical Society collections. Her previous digital library experience includes XSLT style sheet design and markup for the California Digital Library, and project assistantships with the SCAN project at UC Berkeley and the Digital Scriptorium project hosted by Columbia and Berkeley. She has been known to teach AP English and Latin at Holy Child on Long Island.

Art Rhyno

Art Rhyno is the head of the Leddy Library's Systems Department at the University of Windsor. He also holds an adjunct appointment at the Queen Elizabeth II Library at Memorial University of Newfoundland. Art graduated with a degree in math and computer science in 1985 and completed his master's in library and information science in 1988. He has worked on library systems, Web gateways, Java applications, freenets, VRML worlds, and open-source software. Art is a past president of the Ontario Library Information Technology Association (OLITA), and contributes to the Technical Planning Group of Windsor Public Library.

Gail Richardson

Gail Richardson received her M.L.S. degree from the University of Toronto in 1996, following a brief career in administration at the university. In 1997 she founded SGL Information Services, a small group of professional librarians with expertise in managing and delivering information over the Internet. Since 1998 she has been under contract with Halton Hills Public Library as an electronics resource librarian, continuing to work on digitization projects within the library, and as a freelance Web consultant.

Brian Rosenblum

Brian Rosenblum is electronic publishing specialist at the Scholarly Publishing Office, University of Michigan Library. He holds a master's degree from the University of Michigan School of Information, and a master's degree in English from the Claremont Graduate School.

Heidi Schmidt

Heidi Schmidt is the Director of Academic Information Systems in the Library/Center for Knowledge Management at the University of California San Francisco. A relative newcomer to the library environment, she has 15 years of experience supporting information technology in higher education.

Lloyd Sokvitne

Lloyd Sokvitne is the manager of information systems development for the State Library of Tasmania. Lloyd graduated with a Graduate Diploma in librarianship from Kuring-gai CAE, Sydney, Australia, in 1977 and has been employed by the State Library of Tasmania since 1978. At the State Library, Lloyd has worked in cataloging, collection development, and library systems. Since 1995 Lloyd has overseen the development of Tasmania Online (www.tas.gov.au), a comprehensive Tasmanian Web indexing service, which became the Tasmanian State Government Web portal in 1997; Service Tasmania Online (www.service.tas.gov.au), the unified cross-jurisdictional government services portal for Tasmania; and Our Digital Island (www.statelibrary.tas.gov.au/odi), a Web site repository and preservation service. Lloyd's professional interests center on information discovery on the Web, government information services delivery, metadata, and Web content preservation.

Theo van Veen

Theo van Veen was born in 1953, received a degree in physics in 1979, did some years of research on auditory perception, and started working in the area of information and communication technology in 1984. He began working in libraries in 1988 as head of automation at the University Library Utrecht. Now he works as project leader at the Koninklijke Bibliotheek in The Hague.

About the Editor

Roy Tennant is eScholarship Web and services design manager for the California Digital Library. Prior to this, he created and managed the Berkeley Digital Library SunSITE, which is both a digital library and a support service for other digital library developers (http://sunsite.berkeley.edu).

He is the author of *Practical HTML: A Self-Paced Tutorial* and co-author of *Crossing the Internet Threshold: An Instructional Handbook*. His articles have appeared in numerous library and information technology magazines and journals, and he has written the monthly column "Digital Libraries" for *Library Journal* since November 1997. Roy is frequently asked to speak at library conferences around the world, and is noted for his ability to make technical topics understandable to beginners.

The founder and manager of the Web4Lib and XML4Lib electronic discussions, Roy also created and edits the current-awareness publication *Current Cites*, which has been published monthly for well over a decade.

Roy holds a master's degree in library and information studies from the University of California, Berkeley, and a B.A. in geography from Humboldt State University.

His other profession is white-water river guiding, which has provided him with the opportunity of running many of California's raftable rivers as well as leading a half dozen trips down the Colorado River through the Grand Canyon.